T0327905

SUNRISE GRATITUDE

365 MORNING MEDITATIONS
FOR JOYFUL DAYS
ALL YEAR LONG

EMILY SILVA

ROCK
POINT

To my dad, who rose before the sun when I was a child and continues to welcome each day with gratitude, joy, and wonder.

Introduction

GOOD MORNING! For most of my life, I was not a morning person.
It took me a long time to wake up and find my bearings. I wouldn't find
my groove until around noon. Nights were when I was most creative.
The ideas came to me and I could easily stay up late, writing and dreaming.

Then something shifted, and I started to enjoy my mornings. I find the
stillness before the day begins to be a time of contemplation, silence,
and beauty. I love the way the morning light plays with the sky. I love
the feeling of the world waking up and the start of a new day. Beginnings
always feel fresh and exciting. Each morning holds such promise.

In this book, I want to provide you with encouragement, inspiration, and
something to think about each day. Mornings are a time of expansion.
As we fill our lungs with air and move our limbs, we go from the state of
rest and sleep to being fully awake. I thought about readers who are tired
and discouraged, as well as readers who jump out of bed ready to seize the
day. I wanted these passages to bring balance and mindfulness to you.

No matter where you find yourself on the "morning person" scale, I hope
you find something in these pages that inspires and moves you. May your
mornings be a time of mindful solitude. As you transition from rest to
movement, take a moment to just be. You have the rest of the day to take
action and make things happen. Giving yourself the gift of stillness each
morning will help you start the day on a more peaceful note.

As I sit facing the window and look toward the ocean, I notice the sun
slowly rising behind me. The sky is brightening and the marine layer that
loves to sit still until midmorning is becoming illuminated. Seagulls are
singing their morning songs and the air is crisp. I am pausing to offer my
sunrise gratitude for this opportunity and for you, the reader: thank you
for choosing this book as part of your journey.

Emily Silva
San Diego

January 1

START TODAY WITH AN OPEN HEART and fresh eyes. Today has no mistakes in it. Embrace this clean slate by breathing in this present moment of newness, of possibility, and of hope. Nothing but what is happening right now matters. Yesterday is over and today stands before you without expectation. Take a moment to offer gratitude for this day. You have the power to choose the energy you bring to the day.

January 2

WISDOM COMES TO THOSE WHO SEIZE the lessons that life has to offer. Each lesson carries its own level of difficulty, and when it's completed, embrace a sense of relief. Everything you are going through is just part of your path to wisdom. As you enter the new day, look with fresh eyes for what is ready to be learned. Embrace today with open arms and know that your level of understanding is deepening.

———

January 3

SUNRISE IS SUCH A BEAUTIFUL EVENT. To think that the Earth rotated around the sun long enough to offer a sunrise every day is amazing. When you awake before the sun, you are fortunate to be able to catch the first light of a new day. As dawn arises, notice the colors of everything that is becoming illuminated. Notice how you awaken as the light enters your eyes. Breathe in appreciation for the opportunity to experience the exquisiteness of another sunrise.

January 4

APPROACH EACH DAY WITH A SENSE OF WONDER and excitement. Today is an adventure, one you've never been on before. There is always something new to learn, someone new to encounter, and something new to see. Even if your days seem pretty routine, embrace the elements of the unknown. Notice the tiny mysteries each day holds and become an explorer filled with awe as you enter your day. With eyes open toward wonder, it's amazing what you will discover!

———

January 5

THERE IS NOTHING LIKE A FRESH CUP OF COFFEE or tea in the morning. It is a slow ritual to begin the day. It is satisfying to wait for the water to brew the grounds or tea leaves to seep to create the perfect cup. If we can wait for perfection in a cup each morning, why do we get so impatient with the bigger things in life? If you are in a period of waiting, take a deep breath and know that good things take time.

January 6

WHEN YOU AWAKEN, take a moment to do a scan of your body. Notice any places where tension may be and breathe into each one. Feel your breath fill you as it relieves the tension. Allow the oxygen to reach all the way to your fingers and toes. Notice how you feel after each breath. Take this bodily awareness into your day and be grateful for your body and the wonderful miracle it is to be alive.

———

January 7

EVEN THE SMALLEST THINGS CAN make an impact. On the day you were born, you changed someone's life. You are a miracle and the world is more lovely with you in it. Everything about you is special, from your smile to the way you think. Your soul is here to illuminate and shine in its own extraordinary way. Accept everything about yourself, because there is no one else quite like you. You are awesome. You are loved.

January 8

OPPORTUNITY IS ALL AROUND. Look for it and you will
see that there is never a shortage of things to do or places
to go. An abundant mindset sees life as full of choices.
If you feel as if things are lacking, watch your thoughts. Your
perception creates your reality. Every time you notice scarce
thoughts creeping in, stop and find something positive to
center your attention on. You can train your mind toward
abundance and loosen your grip on thoughts about scarcity.

———

January 9

IT'S DIFFICULT TO FOCUS WHEN life seems to be going
in several directions and your home or office is in disarray.
Take some time to clear the clutter in your life. Is there
anything you can let go of, organize, or complete? When we
clear clutter, we create space for peace and calm to enter
our lives. We release any hold we may have on objects or
projects and permit what needs to be in our lives the space
to enter. Letting go is an act of freedom. What will you
release today?

January 10

WHEN YOU OPEN YOUR EYES in the morning, what is the first thing you do? Whatever it is, it sets the tone for your entire day. Those few moments upon waking are very important as we transition from sleeping to waking. Start each day from a place of intention. Provide gratitude, say "I love you" to yourself or partner, and spend a few moments in stillness to set an intention for your day. Create the momentum you desire before you get up as you revel in the stillness of these few early moments.

January 11

IT CAN BE DIFFICULT TO GET UP after experiencing a loss. Facing the day seems daunting. Emotions are high and staying in and away from others may feel safer than dealing with them. When we lose someone or something it is natural to withdraw. There are people who care and want to be there for you. Let them in. Ask for help and the support you need. New beginnings are awaiting you and you don't have to face them alone.

January 12

WHEN A MISUNDERSTANDING OCCURS, respond in love. Love heals. Communicate from the heart with loving intent. Don't worry about the other person's response—just give love. Do your best not to take things personally, knowing that everyone is fighting their own battles inside. Healing occurs where love resides. To live from your whole heart means to soften your emotions and let compassion and love fill the spaces where negative emotions tend to grow. Be vulnerable, open, and loving.

———

January 13

WINTER MORNINGS ARE EXTRA COZY as the sun takes its time to creep over the horizon. Darkness lingers and it feels so nice to stay in bed just a little bit longer. While you prepare for your day, take a moment to appreciate the sleep you just had and the comfort of your bed. As you venture outside, notice the sun's rays peeking through the darkness as it slowly brightens the day. Today is going to be great.

January 14

TAKE SOME TIME TODAY to move your body. Our bodies are a gift and it is important to take care of them. We can choose to move in so many ways; find what works best for you and spend the time to give your body some love and movement. Your mind will thank you by becoming clearer too. It is easy to stay put, but movement makes the day feel richer, our bodies feel stronger, and our minds more aware. How will you move today?

January 15

AS THE SUN RISES OVER THE MOUNTAINS, the world begins to wake up. The day's first light illuminates the dew on each blade of grass, creating a fresh beginning to the day. Flowers begin opening to greet the sun, their blooms moving with the sun throughout the day. As you stir from sleep, turn your face to the sun and take in the goodness of the morning. Notice how new everything looks, well rested and ready for a beautiful day.

January 16

IF THERE IS SOMETHING YOU REALLY WANT, take some time to break it down into baby steps. Ask yourself: "What is one thing I can do today to get closer to my goal?" Then ask yourself that question every day. Before you know it, you're halfway to your goal. Remember that every action is worthy of gratitude and respect because you are choosing to do something to reach a goal instead of doing what is simple or comfortable.

———

January 17

WHEN WE EXPERIENCE CHAOS, it feels as if the world is crumbling all around us. Internally, it can feel like our lives are falling apart. Our outer world is a reflection of our inner world. Chaos scatters and disperses things in new places. After it leaves, things feel misplaced and sometimes lost. Allow things to fall where they may and embrace the new order of things. Surrender the need to control. Accept what is. Everything is exactly where it needs to be.

January 18

THE REST YOU JUST HAD PREPARED YOU for today. Our bodies are intelligent and know when to sleep and when to wake up. It's amazing that we walk around with such inherent intelligence as our bodies do the work to regulate and propel us forward. Be thankful for the body you have and for the systems that guide our sleep, digestion, movement, and feeling. It's a blessing. Do something to show your body appreciation today. You deserve to treat yourself with care.

January 19

POSSIBILITY IS THE CORE OF DREAMING, and when we concentrate on the potential each day brings, we allow hope to grow. Each day holds so many options! Opportunities will appear depending on where we choose to pay attention. If you are wondering why life seems limited, change your perspective. Notice where your concentration lies. In order for life to present the possibilities you desire, you must take your attention there. By shifting your energy and perspective, new horizons will appear.

January 20

THE SUN GLISTENS UP IN THE SKY as the marvel of
the night dims away. And yet, everything in the universe
is still there, despite the veil of a blue sky and a bright
sun. The stars are still shining and the moon continues its
orbit. Nothing stops. This realization is amazing and allows
for perspective when troubles seem too big. If an entire
universe can carry on when the sun rises, so can you.
Rise up. Do your best to seize the day.

January 21

HUMPBACK WHALES MIGRATE up and down the coast
every year. In the winter, they search for warmer waters.
By instinct, they follow their inner compass and temperature
changes of the ocean. It's amazing that they know where
and when to go. We too have an inner compass that guides
us through life. If we take the time to listen for the subtle
cues of our intuition, we can learn to trust our instincts at
a deeper level. Take a moment to be still and welcome the
wisdom of your intuition.

January 22

YOU HAVE A SPIRIT OF FIRE within you. It is the light that shines within. It fuels your passion and keeps you going when you know something is important. Each morning, you have the chance to calibrate your light as the sun rises. Imagine your inner fire rising within. Will it be a bright flame that burns slowly and evenly or a burst of energy, creating a shock of illumination? Our lights may differ every day, but they never go out.

———

January 23

WAKING UP FROM A DREAM can be a wonderful thing. Our dreams are portals into our subconscious, and upon waking we have a chance to capture what we experienced in sleep. This morning, think about the dreams you just had and write them down. Notice any clues they may have for you. We don't have to wait until sleep to live in a dream. If you want something, take action today. Every small step leads to change.

January 24

ASKING FOR HELP IS A SIGN of strength. Knowing when you need assistance and letting down your guard to ask for what you need takes humility and strength. You are a humble warrior, ready to take on the day yet bowing in respect for those who have helped you. Great things are accomplished with help and guidance. There is always a wealth of wisdom to draw from. Open your heart and mind to growth and know that each person you meet has the potential to be a teacher.

January 25

START YOUR DAY WITH THESE affirming words: *My heart is full of love. I will let someone know that I love them today. When I express love, I improve my mood and bring higher energy to those I love. Many people have made an impact on my life and I appreciate their presence. When I feel a positive emotion or thought about someone today, I will let them know to spread love. My day will be brighter through spreading love.*

January 26

PROTECT YOUR ENERGY. It's easy to absorb the energy of others. If something dulls your spirit, walk away, shift the attention, or let it go. Energy vampires can be people, activities, or the food and media we consume. To live a vibrant life, choose the things that light you up and raise your energy. When you recognize when your energy is being drained, you can become more aware of your needs. Surround yourself with what brings you peace, joy, and vitality.

January 27

HAPPINESS COMES FROM cultivating a spirit of contentment. You are exactly where you need to be. All of the things you wish for may come, but for right now, everything you need has been provided. Look at your life knowing that everything is as it should be. Breathe in this truth and find peace knowing that all is well. Lift your arms to the sky with gratitude. Feel your heart swell with appreciation and attract happiness by choosing to be content.

January 28

WE CAN'T WAIT FOR OTHER PEOPLE'S validation to move forward. The power to make something happen lies within each of us. When we acknowledge our inner source of power, great things occur. You have the ability to create and you don't need anyone's permission or approval to act. When we create an expectation about how another person will act, we set ourselves up for disappointment and in turn become frozen as we wait. Trust yourself and move forward.

January 29

WAKING UP TO A BLANKET OF fresh snow is a remarkable and peaceful sight. Everything feels cozier and the world seems hushed. Snow is like a fresh slate, covering everything in white. Even the soil underneath lies dormant, waiting for the warmth of spring. It's okay to have periods of rest. Everything needs time to recharge. If you need stillness, allow yourself to be still. Just as the Earth goes through seasons, so do our bodies. Be kind to yourself today!

January 30

REMEMBER WHEN YOU WERE SMALL and wanted so badly to grow up? Childhood is filled with milestones; we are measured and tested. As adults, we tend to put aside a focus on growth and merely adapt to how we see things, believing that our state is permanent. This morning, challenge yourself to see things through the eyes of your younger self. Remember the hope and possibility you had. Infuse your day with wonder and see that nothing is permanent—and anything is possible.

January 31

WHEN YOU'RE FEELING OVERWHELMED, it's important to breathe. Sometimes we get too caught up in the task at hand and forget our most basic need: oxygen. Take a break and do nothing. We all need time to recharge. If we keep going nonstop, it can lead to burn-out and then we will be forced to rest. Rest should be a beautiful choice and a present you give yourself. Abandon the need to do and be everything and allow yourself peace and relaxation.

February 1

OUT IN THE OCEAN, dolphins ride the waves alongside surfers. They are playful and curious. Swimming in pods, they take turns jumping and flipping through the water, looking like they don't have a care in the world. Be like a dolphin and infuse more play into your life. Jump in puddles, laugh out loud, ride a bike, learn to surf! Choose to open your mind to the more playful and curious side of yourself. Life is your playground.

February 2

WANTING MORE THAN WHAT YOU HAVE causes anxiety, feelings of inadequacy, and invites thoughts of scarcity into your mind. When we operate from a place of contentment, we feel abundant and joyful. Everything you need is on its way to you. What you have right now is exactly what you need. Our deepest desires are heard and sometimes we get the answer of "not right now." Trust that answer and the timing in your life. Your needs will be provided.

February 3

AFTER A COLD NIGHT, the ground is crystalized with a blanket of frost. This shimmering, icy layer can keep us from moving quickly and rushing through our mornings. Frost is an invitation to mindfully enter your morning unrushed. As the ice melts, be grateful for the warm bed you slept in and the beauty of a winter morning. Allow gratitude to enter if frustration may be bubbling up. Winter is a time to rest and move slower. Take a cue from nature and allow the day to progress without rushing.

February 4

MORNINGS PROVIDE THE FEELING of freshness. The air smells clean and feels like a new beginning. The dew left on the ground glistens like a shiny new object. Everything is renewed and fresh. As you awaken, feel the renewal that sleep provided. Be present with this feeling. Nothing else matters in this moment. Be here now, ready to take on the new day that has dawned. Right now is your chance to begin again. Let go of all worries and regrets. Today you have the gift of a fresh start.

February 5

EVERY PERSON YOU MEET has a mixture of stories full of happiness and sorrow. You never know what a person is celebrating or mourning with just a glance. As we get to know each other, our complexity reveals itself. Offer compassion to every person you encounter, for they too have a deep soul. If someone rubs you the wrong way, send them love. They may need it more than ever. Stop judgments as they appear; they are only a reflection of your inner world.

February 6

BIG DECISIONS CAN SEEM SCARY, but that fear can be from anticipation and not dread. Anticipation triggers hope, excitement, anxiety, and doubt all in one moment. If you've really gone over the options and know the answer but can't seem to make that jump, harness your bravery to jump with confidence. Courage requires confidence. Believe in your decisions. Trust your intuition. You won't know what's waiting on the other side of the decision until you move forward. Be brave and know that everything will be okay.

February 7

GOING AFTER WHAT YOU WANT is an opportunity to honor your soul and take action toward fulfillment. If you have a desire in your heart, you have the choice to do what it takes to make it happen. When you decide to go after a dream, be prepared for the work it takes to make it come true. It will be all worth it in the end. Welcome the hard work it takes for your life to change.

———

February 8

BE DILIGENT IN THE PURSUIT OF your dreams. If you find yourself feeling disgruntled at the work involved, think about the honeybee and how it works hard for a sweet reward. Changing your perspective on work can create different results in your mind and body. Some tasks are inevitable and necessary to get to the next level. See that you are part of a bigger picture and that your reward is on its way.

February 9

IN SOFTNESS, WE OPEN UP to possibility, hope, and creation. You are the master creator of your life, and your hopes and dreams are meant to become a reality. There is no need to hold on tight. Allow space for what's meant to leave so what's meant to be can fill the space. When your dreams come to fruition, hold gratitude deep in your heart, because you created and believed in your possibility. Soften into your newfound success and into greater trust in yourself.

February 10

GOING THROUGH A PAINFUL PERIOD can feel isolating. It feels as if no one understands or knows the right thing to say. Eventually, joy finds its way back. It can show up in the kindness of a friend or a gorgeous sunrise. Slowly, it creeps back into your soul. Absorb each small moment of joy. Those moments will become easier to recognize and you may find yourself blessing the pain you went through when joy finds its way back into your heart.

February 11

THROUGH PERSISTENCE, we step into our greatness. It takes hard work, dedication, and practice to embrace our fullest potential. We need times of rest and compassion throughout this process. Don't let perfectionism take over. Give yourself compassion when things don't go as planned. Rest when you find yourself feeling burned out. You are meant for great things and each step you take brings you closer to your potential. Acknowledge all the work you've done with pride. Give yourself credit for all you have done. You are amazing!

February 12

THE JOY YOU HAVE NOW is in part a result of all the pain you have overcome. Because you were tried, hurt, sad, and angry—and chose to rise above it—you can experience life on a richer level. You went through the valley to reach a summit. You fought for your joy, so revel in it. Let it wash over you. Feel gratitude at a cellular level, because you have softened from the pain and your heart is more open than ever before.

February 13

DEEP IN THE OCEAN there are mysteries yet to be discovered. The wisdom in these depths are available, even without us finding them. In stillness, we find the answers that lie deep inside us. Our souls speak when we drown out all distractions, patiently waiting for us to find solitude so that we can connect. In this quiet space, our anxious minds find peace and connection to the part of ourselves that is greater than any problem we face.

February 14

WHEN SOMETHING FEELS IMPOSSIBLE, it may take some time to find your way. We are prone to react in frustration when things seem difficult. But from this perspective, the natural response is to give up. Giving up doesn't get you closer to your goal and will leave you even more frustrated. Instead, take a breath and revisit the issue once you've cleared your head, so you can have a renewed outlook. Take action from this place of calm and not from a place of reaction.

February 15

IN SHADE, IVY CREEPS its way up the trunk of an olive tree. It clings tightly to the tree, spinning its way around the trunk. The tree does not hinder the growth of the ivy; it just stands tall, offering shade while staying rooted in its own growth. If you are offering support to someone, stay rooted in your own growth. Take time to replenish yourself and care for your own needs. Then you can be the supportive person you want to be.

February 16

WE CAN ALWAYS FIND SOMETHING to be grateful for. Think about the best thing that is happening right now. No matter what is going wrong, find the positive and center your attention on it. Life will throw wrenches in our plans; things will fall apart, and timing isn't always on our side. But there is always something to be grateful for, even if it's buried under all the challenges. Find the joy in today and exude the joy it provides. Feel deep gratitude and smile.

February 17

A GREAT LESSON FROM A RIVER is to be fluid and let things come and go. Holding on causes a lot of suffering, including bitterness, resentment, sorrow, and anger, to name a few. When you choose to let go of your reaction to hurt, you will feel freer to pay attention to the beautiful things in life. Sometimes it can feel comforting to commiserate, but catch yourself, because you can always focus on something more positive. Nothing is worth diverting attention away from the good things that life has to offer.

February 18

SOMETIMES LIFE FEELS LIKE being caught in a tornado. Mornings can be especially difficult when we have so many things to do and take care of. But a tornado loses its power eventually. Its centrifugal force unwinds and there is calm after the storm. If you are feeling wound up this morning, take the time to unwind. Our mornings set the tone for our day. Instead of entering the day spinning, take extra time to find calm.

February 19

SNOW DAYS OR COLD DAYS ARE THE PERFECT time
to do nothing for the sake of nothingness. There is an art to
doing nothing, especially with all the distractions available.
It's normal to want to distract ourselves with something
when nothing is exactly what we need. When you're feeling
overwhelmed, tired, or overstimulated, do nothing. Sit with
your thoughts. When the weather keeps you from going
anywhere, permit boredom to set in. In this space, clarity
can surface. In this space, your mind and spirit can reset.

———

February 20

LIVING INTENTIONALLY CREATES a soulful reason
behind our actions. When we take the time to zero in
on what we want and why we want it, we can narrow in on
our purpose. Instead of allowing our thoughts to run wild,
focusing shapes our reality. Wherever our focus goes,
growth can take place. Creating an intention with focus
will reap rewards. In fact, it may not happen exactly as
you would envision, but it will happen as it should.

February 21

WHEN YOU ARE GOING THROUGH A HARD TIME, the feeling of sorrow can seem impermeable. Finding the light at the end of the tunnel seems like a daunting task and our minds may become paralyzed in hopelessness. But there is an end. The sun always rises and hard times do pass. Create space and allow your soul to renew. Some things in your life may no longer serve you. Bless them and open your arms wide for the incoming blessings.

February 22

EARLY IN THE MORNING THE OCEAN IS CALM, reflecting the sun's rising gleam. Suddenly, the water parts as a humpback whale jumps out of the ocean, twisting its massive body, disrupting the peaceful scene. To observe a whale breaching is to be left in wonder. Nature is full of moments that inspire a spirit of awe. To observe such wonder, stay in the moment. Let nature's glamour take your breath away. Moments of wonder are waiting to be discovered every day.

February 23

A TREE SWAYS IN THE WIND, its leaves dancing with the breeze. It doesn't seem bothered by the wind's power; it simply bends and moves with the current. Life is full of changes, and if we don't accept them as they come about, we can break like branches that don't sway with the wind. Learning to be flexible creates acceptance of whatever life offers. Learn to sway like a tree, to stay open and flexible. Sometimes the unexpected parts of life are the most beautiful.

———

February 24

REPEAT THESE AFFIRMATIONS to begin your day:

I am a student of life. I will continue to learn lessons every day. I am excited to see what this day will teach me. I will approach this day like a student in class and lean into the lessons. The more I open my mind to learning something new, the quicker I will find understanding and peace when difficulties arise. I am becoming more resilient and wise. When I imagine what a lifetime can teach me, I am fascinated.

February 25

IN THE REDWOODS A SILENCE PERMEATES the ancient forest. Walking among these giant trees inspires looking up and realizing how small we really are. The same can be said of some of our problems. When we look past our perception, we can notice how small the problems may be. If something is troubling you today, spend some time in silence. Allow the discomfort to unfold in peace. Find one thing you can do to alleviate your pain. Perhaps spend some time with the trees and be enveloped in peace.

February 26

YOUR HEART EXPANDS THE MORE YOU LOVE—and you have so much love to give. When your feelings are hurt, forgive. Don't hold on to the pain, because it only hurts you, and your heart is intended to love. Relinquish the weight of opinions and judgments and give grace to yourself and others. Have courage and trust that you are here for a reason. Embrace your talents, for there are many. Share your gifts with the world. We need you.

February 27

WAITING FOR SOMETHING CAN BE DIFFICULT,
especially when we are attached to it. When we want
something, we can fixate on it, forgetting everything else
that surrounds us. In times like these, it's important to
remember that everything happens when it's supposed to.
Appreciate your here and now. Anticipate what's ahead, but
also appreciate your current situation. Then when what you
want arrives, your heart and mind will already be calibrated
toward gratitude.

February 28/29

BEAUTIFUL THINGS HAPPEN EVERY DAY. The sun
comes up, a blossom opens, laughter, hugs, and smiles
appear. The list goes on. Center your attention on the
beauty in life. Our perspective shapes our inner world and
creates the energy we give off. If we focus on beauty, we
can't help but see the beauty in each person and in our
surroundings. If you find yourself having negative thoughts
today, stop to notice something beautiful.

March 1

THE SUN SHINES ITS LIGHT ON THE LAKE, making
nature sparkle as it welcomes a new day. Every morning
the water just sits there waiting for the sun to shine. The
two create an incredible greeting to the day. How will you
sparkle today? How can you bring your radiance to things
that seem ordinary? Your light is as glorious as the sun.
Give off light wherever you go.

March 2

IT'S A MIRACLE TO BE ALIVE. Think about how remarkable you are. You have lungs to breathe with, eyes that can read these words, a brain that comprehends, and a soul that feels. Every system in your body is a work of art. What a glorious honor to be a human being with thoughts and feelings. You are a gift to this world. Appreciate each body function and emotion that you experience. Start today with a renewed sense of awe.

March 3

RAIN CLEARS THE AIR from pressure that has been building. Clouds collect water until they are so full a release is unavoidable. Think about all the things you are holding on to in your life. Where is the pressure building? Release whatever you are holding on to and allow the pressure to dissipate. You are in control of feeling the relief. Release it like a rain cloud and feel your spirit become lighter like the air after a storm.

March 4

WHEN YOU WAKE UP, it's like opening a new book. Make your life your favorite story, because it's a lovely story that happens to be true. You are the main character and you get to decide how you would like your story to transpire. You create your reality. Do something today that sets the stage for your story to unfold. As the author of your life, you can change scenes and make anything happen. Don't play small.

March 5

A LIFE OF CONTENTMENT abounds with gratitude. When you feel that things aren't the way they should be, find the things that are. Shift your attention to the positive aspects of life to cultivate a content heart. When contentment grows, our perception of reality changes and the things that used to bother us don't hold much power. Our minds are powerful, and if we focus our attention on gratitude and positive thoughts, contentment is a result. What are you grateful for today?

March 6

EVEN WHEN WE ARE going through a drought, a blossom is just waiting to happen. To bloom, wildflowers don't do anything but receive air, sunlight, and rain. Sometimes we don't need to do anything but trust that what we need is on its way. If you think life isn't going the way you planned, be more like the wildflowers and patiently wait for sunshine and rain. All droughts eventually end and the blessings will come.

March 7

EVERY DAY GIVES US the chance for joy. We wake up with a fresh start and anything is possible. This moment is the only thing that matters. If you feel residue from yesterday, take a moment to loosen its hold on you. Journal it out: get it out of your head and onto paper. Transfer the energy. Today deserves your full attention—and yesterday is over. How can you infuse your day with the energy of joy?

March 8

EARLY IN THE MORNING, you rise before the sun. You look out onto a stunning, still lake and notice the outline of the mountains before the sun creeps its way up to the horizon. You spend these quiet moments in stillness and gratitude. As the sun makes its appearance over the mountains, it illuminates the water, creating a mirror for the sky above. You turn your face toward the sun, determined to make it a great day. Incredible things await you today.

March 9

FOG ROLLS IN AND COVERS THE SHORELINE, shrouding everything in mystery. Like a heavy blanket, it covers everything in its path. Only when you move close enough to something can you see it clearly. There is beauty in mystery and discovery. If you are in a period of wondering, move closer to get a clearer picture. Be patient for things to reveal themselves to you. There is beauty in revelation. When we wait with anticipation, the reveal can feel even more astounding.

March 10

LET HOPE ENTER WHEN DOUBT ARRIVES. Even if you don't know how things will work out, know that the universe hears your deepest desires. Hope and trust can bring lightness to the heaviness of uncertainty. Like a wave coming to shore clearing debris and smoothing the sand, hope can clear the effects of doubt. Allow waves of love, patience, and optimism to enter where thoughts of uncertainty appear. Replace doubt with the hopefulness of a dream come true.

March 11

THE QUEST FOR BALANCE IS UNIVERSAL. Polarities exist and arise, especially when we need to make decisions. A pro and a con can be found for each side. The key is to find a balance where the contrasts coincide. Instead of fighting against each other, find ways that they can work together. Abandon anything that disrupts the balance and build equilibrium when possible. This is a continuous process that requires attention and flow. Flow will help lead you to a more balanced life.

March 12

MORNINGS ARE A SACRED TIME FOR OUR BRAINS.
After we awaken from a night full of dreaming, we have
a choice of allowing our brains to wake up naturally or
consuming by awakening with harsh lights and news. Once
we pick up our devices, we flood our brains with stimulation
and outside opinions. Before this flood happens, spend time
in peace. Breathe in the quiet before your day begins, and if
you feel moved, create something before you pay attention
to the creations of others.

March 13

WHEN CHARGED CONVERSATIONS and comments are
circulating, it's easy to get wrapped up in judgment. But
these vibrations weaken our true soul power. Instead of
joining in from a reactive state, let go of judgments and
spread love, kindness, and understanding. There is a lot of
hurt in this world and healing can be fueled only by higher
vibrational acts like love, kindness, and forgiveness. If you
are in a situation that is painful and reactive, take a moment
to find balance so you can communicate in love. From that
space, healing can take place.

March 14

A FLOWER PUSHES ITS WAY through the soil to bloom. As a seed, it dreams of the gorgeous petals it will display. As it reaches for the sky, its roots and stem stay close to the soil. Be like a flower and dream but stay grounded. It takes bravery and wisdom to dream big while taking steps toward making a leap. Action and planning with a touch of intuitive spark can make life magical.

March 15

EACH BIRD HAS A SONG, and early in the morning birds welcome the day with their breathtaking chorus. Singing high in the trees, they chirp to welcome the rising sun. Have you ever stopped to listen to the chirping of birds? It's beautiful and melodic; each song is different. Take a moment today to pause and hear the birdsong, wherever you are. Notice how many birds are singing along. This mindful act will invite peace into your day.

March 16

ALL YOUR NEEDS ARE BEING MET. The universe always provides. We can easily focus on scarcity when things don't fall into place exactly as we want them to. The need for control creeps in only enhancing the feeling of scarcity. But if you evaluate the situation from a place of calm, there is always enough. Trust that your needs are being met. Ask for provisions and let go. An abundant mindset is not rooted in worry but in trust.

March 17

KNOWING WHAT YOU WANT and going after it is bravery in action. Many things keep us from fulfilling our dreams. We can allow doubt, judgement, and guilt to keep us from moving into the lives we desire. These tendencies mask fear and try to keep us sheltered in what's comfortable. Squash doubt with the confidence that you are following your soul's calling. Reframe judgement into a positive affirmation and release guilt by honoring your journey to greater self-respect.

March 18

WE ARE MEANT TO FIND connection with others. Our minds and hearts flourish when we find connection and belonging. It's an amazing thing to find people who share the same interests and insights as we do. It's also necessary to find people who help us grow. Staying isolated keeps us from thriving and sharing our hearts. Think about the people you have a connection with and take some time to give thanks for each of them. A life with connection is sacred.

March 19

WHEN THE SUN COMES UP over the ocean, it looks as if half of the sun is lingering below the hemisphere, sharing its last rays before illuminating the entire sky. Sometimes our radiance lingers below the surface. At times we feel afraid to shine too brightly and keep our full glow hidden from view. This doesn't help anyone. The world needs your full shine, just as each day needs the entire brightness of the sun. Rise up and shine your astonishing light.

March 20

WE GO NUMB WHEN WE want to avoid something. We do this in many ways. We may shut down or lean into a drama to create a false narrative about what's happening. Drama can be a deterrent from feeling and dealing with core issues. Use stillness to create awareness and then proceed with love and understanding. Take time to learn and grow from these experiences. Find out what the lesson is and lose the desire to go numb and avoid what you need to face head on.

March 21

WHEN THINGS DON'T SEEM TO BE GOING the way you want, you have a choice to make: resist or welcome peace. Resisting causes stress and anxiety. Most of us tend to dwell on how we want things to go and become stressed out. But if you release control, you allow what needs to happen to play out as it's supposed to. Many factors are at work and we can't know how it all fits together yet. Choose to cease resisting and allow peace to enter.

March 22

LOOKING BACK CAN BE a lovely process. Reminiscing about special memories can bring joy and laughter. But when we look back to remind someone of the suffering they've caused or to relive a painful memory, we are harming ourselves and potentially others. Forgive the pain that's buried in the past. Move forward from the wound. Heal what needs to be healed and disconnect from your attachment to any residual pain. Holding on constricts growth. Choose to forgive as many times as you need to.

March 23

MORNING GLORIES OPEN their purple faces to the sun every day. They follow the sun's glimmer and then close as the sun sets. To see a vine full of these flowers can bring us into the present moment. They are so vibrant and abundant. Every day we can turn our face to the sun to invite energy throughout the day, and then take a cue from morning glories to rest at night.

March 24

THE SUN'S ENERGY IS POWERFUL and its heat affects the entire solar system. The fact that the Earth is the perfect distance from the sun to be able to sustain life is fascinating. Knowing that we were born on this planet and receive energy and light from a massive ball of burning gas is awe-inspiring. Spend some time today receiving energy from the sun and reveling in the astonishment of the universe. Offer gratitude for the warmth and life the sun provides.

March 25

NEW BEGINNINGS ARE A TIME for celebration. A seed must be watered in order to sprout. A lot of work occurs below the soil, and when the seedling pushes through the dirt it's a sign of growth. Growth is not a simple process. It can be painful and gritty. Eventually, blossoming occurs. You are growing. If it feels difficult, remember that you too will soon bloom. Allow yourself the time to push through the soil.

March 26

GIVE YOURSELF SOME LOVE today with these words:
I am love. My heart expands as I give love to myself and others. I choose to practice acceptance today and extend grace when needed. I am grateful for the love in my life. Love is an abundant, universal force, and I send it out freely. Just like everyone else, I too desire love and am thankful for the people who love me exactly as I am. Today I offer unconditional love to myself. Love has the power to heal.

March 27

THE WIND IS A POWERFUL FORCE, strong enough to change a landscape. With the help of the wind, sand dunes form and shift. The wind also reminds us that things are constantly changing and that being adaptable is the best way to survive. If we resist, we are only pushing against a force that will eventually move. Suspend the urge to stay put and allow yourself to be moved wherever you're designed to go. Welcome ease into your life by releasing control.

March 28

SOMETIMES WE TAKE THE SIMPLEST things for granted. Imagine if the sun never rose to offer its plentiful light every day. Our bodies would be thrown off, plants would cease to grow, and the air would be quite cold. Spread your arms wide and welcome the sun this morning. Find a sunny patch to sit in and soak up its radiant light. Say a prayer of thanks for the spectacular force that is the sun.

March 29

AS TREES BEGIN TO BUD, their blossoms showcase a burst of color before leaves fill up the branches. For a short time, the blossoms create a canopy with their delicate petals. This short period signals newness and growth. The tree survived the winter and celebrates by showing off its beauty. If you are going through a period of change, remember that change is a beautiful process. You are blossoming and will ultimately feel the fullness of this transition.

March 30

TO LIVE IN TRUTH, one must speak truth. What have you been needing to say? Is communication tough in a certain situation? When the throat chakra, our energetic center of communication, is blocked, it can be difficult to communicate our truth. Take a moment to breathe calming, healing light into your throat. Write out the truth. Practice speaking it. Permit the blockage the time it needs to dissipate. If the narrative needs healing or rewriting, pay attention. Communicate when the time feels right. Be loving toward your truth.

————

March 31

A MORNING RITUAL IS a great way to begin each day. It is essential to your self-care to take time to create space for yourself. A ritual can be as long or as short as you like. Come up with a list of things that must happen for you to feel your best. In time, your morning routine will become a habit. With consistency, you will find a sense of motivation and calm because you are taking time to set yourself up for success every day.

April 1

LIFE HOLDS SO MANY SIMPLE PLEASURES! To wake up and take a breath, to hear the lovely sounds of the morning, to feel the warmth of the rising sun, to smell fresh coffee and toasted bread—all pockets of delight that each day brings. Our senses are coming alive as we awaken. Take a moment to be grateful for each sense and notice what you are feeling as you open your eyes to welcome the day. Take in the experience of feeling truly alive and grateful.

———

April 2

LIFE BRINGS ENDLESS ADVENTURES. When we choose to take risks, our story can take a turn for better or for worse. That is the nature of risks: the outcome is unknown. If you want your life to be more rewarding, some risk will be involved. Is there something you have been wanting to do? Is there someplace you want to go? Take the risk and accept the adventure of being alive.

April 3

YOU ARE THE LEADER OF YOUR LIFE. You get to decide the way it will go. Don't give your power away by waiting for someone else to provide direction. The power to choose and create lies within you, and when you harness those powers, your life becomes a work of art. What do you choose today? What do you want to create? Take action to move toward the vision of the life you desire. Be the leader you were born to be and choose to create.

April 4

DEEP AT THE BOTTOM OF THE GRAND CANYON, the Colorado River rushes through with powerful energy. For years the river carved its way through, forming one of the most stunning sights on Earth. Rivers change things because they flow, even when it means breaking down hard surfaces. If you are feeling resistance, be like a river and allow life to flow by letting go of the need to control.

April 5

AN ACT OF KINDNESS can brighten the day of a stranger. When we give, we also receive the gift of joy. Think about a time when you gave from your heart. Do you remember the way it made you feel? Now think about a time when you randomly received something. How did the surprise change your day? Think of a way you can deliver a random act of kindness today to infuse the day with happiness.

———

April 6

ON SOME MORNINGS IT IS HARDER than on others to be motivated. So many factors can keep us from feeling our best, for instance, the lack of sleep. Be gentle with yourself and know that it's okay to feel off from time to time. Don't think of yourself as wrong for a lack of motivation. Instead, zero in on why you don't feel motivated, and try to work from there. Find one thing you can do to change your energy. Even a small effort is progress.

April 7

TO TRULY GIVE AND RECEIVE LOVE, we must try to love ourselves. It's amazing how our critical mind quiets when we flood it with approval and love. Try to catch the negative thoughts as they come and replace them with love and approval. It's a practice—and just trying makes a difference. When we come from a place of self-compassion and acceptance, it's easier to put ourselves out there to others. Affirm yourself when negative self-talk arises. You deserve kind words and acceptance.

April 8

WHEN DOUBT FILLS YOUR MIND, stop and remember that the answer is ready to be discovered. Your soul is your inner compass and when you spend time in solitude and contemplation, the answer will appear. Your intuition is a well of wisdom and is always available to you. Doubt is just fear trying to sneak its way into your mind and keep you from moving forward. You know better—and stillness will help you summon the strength to loosen fear's grip.

April 9

WHEN A BABY IS BORN, development takes time.
It is an amazing and intricate process to go from infancy
to adulthood. Growth takes time. The same is true for
our intentions. Look back three months and recall what your
intentions were. Acknowledge where you are now. If you
believe growth isn't happening, ask yourself what you can
do differently to encourage growth. Bless the process and
know that even with minor strides, growth is taking place.

April 10

THINK ABOUT YOUR FAVORITE PLACE in nature and
how it makes you feel. It's important to feed our souls by
removing ourselves from everyday life and connecting with
our inner animal. Each of us has a spirit that is awakened by
being in nature. Enable your wild side to be nurtured by its
innate need to be in a natural environment. The mountains,
desert, ocean, hills, lakes, and trees are calling. Where will
you go to awaken your spirit?

April 11

WHAT'S ONE THING YOU'VE ALWAYS wanted to do but haven't found time to do yet? Now visualize yourself doing just that. What does it feel like? You can make it happen! Write out the actions you need to take to develop this reality. Create progress by showing up for your vision. Move in that direction every day. Small steps equal progress, and progress takes time, so be patient with your process. Slow and steady and you can make a dream come true.

April 12

STRIVING FOR BALANCE CAN FEEL like an uphill battle, one that never reaches a summit. As we strive to balance life, we often become even more imbalanced. There will be times when certain areas in our lives demand more attention than others. When this happens, instead of stressing out about balance, strive to bring grace and understanding to the situation and the process. Life has ups and downs. Bless the highs and lows: they are what make life such a magnificent journey.

April 13

BEGINNINGS CREATE A FRESH perspective and a sense of excitement. Think about what it would feel like if you entered each day with enthusiasm and newness. By putting your attention on the day ahead, possibilities can feel endless. When we take our thoughts away from yesterday and enter each day with a fresh start, we allow life to surprise and delight us. Challenge yourself to find something new each day. Turn your awareness to the present moment and begin again.

April 14

THE FEELING OF BEING ENOUGH and accepting who you are is powerful. It can be scary to wholeheartedly accept yourself. But that's only because important things tend to scare us before we do them. When you are having difficulty accepting yourself, ask: What is one thing I can do today to accept myself? Even small acts move you toward full acceptance. Reframe the thoughts that deny self-approval and cultivate self-love step by step.

April 15

PEACE COMES WHEN WE INVITE it in like a welcome guest. As peace enters our soul, we feel an expansion where anxiety and sorrow once were. When peace arrives, we feel lighter. To prepare your soul for peace, take the time to breathe, clearing the clutter of your mind and opening to the expansion of your spirit. Welcome peace in by releasing the tight grasp of anxiety and sorrow. Let go of pain so that peace can soothe.

April 16

THERE IS TIME TO BE MINDFUL EVERY DAY. Take the time to still your mind and find your breath. Connect with the oxygen flowing through your body. Notice any areas that feel tense and the thoughts that appear. Appreciate your body for its intricate design and important functions. Start your day being mindfully grateful for your body. From this place, you can enter your day with an open mind and heart, ready to show up in your greatest capacity.

April 17

THE ACT OF GENEROSITY brings abundance into your life. When you are generous you are telling the universe "Thank you for the good in my life; I feel blessed and want to share the goodness that's been provided." The energy we emit comes back to us. Generosity does not only mean monetary giving. We can be generous with our time, our talents, and our love. When we give with an open heart, we are operating from a place of abundance.

April 18

WALKING IN THE WOODS is a wonderful way to connect with the primal energy within us. We are meant to get in touch with the natural world. Nature is a wonderful stress reliever. Standing among trees gives us perspective on just how small we are and how vast the universe is. Our problems are not greater than we are. We are greater than the trials we go through. When you are feeling overwhelmed, seek out nature to connect with a power greater than your worries.

April 19

WHEN PEOPLE PASS AWAY, those who are left behind feel
the loss. Our energy leaves a legacy after we pass. How does
your energy leave people feeling? Are you bringing your highest
energy forward? We have the power to raise our vibrations and
in turn attract like energy to us. As you go through your day,
catch yourself when your energy dips or a negative thought
surfaces. Take the time to reframe it and shift your energy from
low to high. Bring the energy you want to receive.

———

April 20

WHEN YOU FIND YOURSELF DISAPPOINTED, try to find
something to be grateful for. Life is full of opportunities to
reframe negative emotions, and the more we practice finding
the positive, the easier it will be to do this. We can train our
minds to be more positive because our minds are malleable.
Don't allow yourself to become stuck in a whirlwind of
disappointment. Pull yourself out of the spiral of negativity
by finding the good in each situation.

April 21

IF YOU WANT CHANGE TO OCCUR, you must do something about it. Like a caterpillar goes through the process of creating a cocoon, you too can do the hard work to create the transformation you desire. Success doesn't happen overnight; a process is required. Do something every day that serves your desired result. Each stride will change you just a little and prepare you for what's next. Eventually you will emerge, like a caterpillar from the chrysalis, transformed and more vibrant.

April 22

ALLOW YOURSELF THE SPACE each day to find wonder in the ordinary. We are likely to go through our days on autopilot and forget to notice what's around. Sometimes we even forget to breathe. Take time to do your activities mindfully. Notice what your senses take in as you do the activity. Take your time and go from mindless to mindful. Then see if you can find some wonder in the task. When we look for wonder, it's amazing how it reveals itself.

April 23

OUR FRIENDSHIPS ARE SOULFUL gifts to be cherished.
Each of us has a soul, and when we feel connection it's
an indicator that our souls have found someone else's soul
friendly. Not everyone connects, and that is okay. Friendship
is supposed to feel connected, joyful, and supportive. If you
are craving more soulful connections, be what you want to
attract, and you will find likeminded souls. When you do find
a connection, nurture it with care.

April 24

IT'S DIFFICULT TO BE BRAVE, especially when there are
so many unknowns swirling about. If you crave security
and certainty, one of the greatest things you can do is learn
to welcome uncertainty. Uncertainty creates a new level
of fear that you can transform into trust. Trust that all your
efforts are being met by the universe and that things will
eventually fall into place. Visualize the outcome you desire
and surrender. Freedom and wonder are on the other side
of letting go.

April 25

START THE DAY by repeating these affirmations to yourself:
*I am talented and capable. I enter this day ready to create change
and contribute to my success. When I doubt myself, I will release
the need to know everything. I have the ability to solve problems.
Nothing is too difficult, and I know how to use my resources.
There is a wealth of knowledge within me and I am open
to learning and developing my skills. Today is the perfect day to
learn something new, because I am capable of great things.*

———

April 26

RAIN IS A SYMBOL OF washing away the old so that growth
can occur. Rain cleanses and nourishes as well as destroys.
Depending on the force and timing, rain can be a welcomed
friend or a feared enemy. Nature is full of duality. What can
seem good to some can be bad to others. It's all about the
meaning we attribute to something. The same can go for our
words and deeds. Choose to live life with the best intentions
and offer nourishment instead of negativity.

April 27

IF YOU ARE FEELING THAT LIFE is stale and you are craving change, get out of your comfort zone and do something different. You have the power to create the life you want. Listen to the longing of your soul and do something to move toward that desire. Start today! Write down everything you want to do and the actions you need to take. Then choose one thing you can do to start the process. Don't just dream it, do it!

April 28

SLOW DOWN. Don't allow yourself to fall into the trap of glorifying busy-ness. Life is intended to be savored and this moment is the most important. Move through your day consciously. Notice the little things and expand your awareness. Flowers bloom for only a season; children grow up fast; and the leaves change and eventually fall. Savor what's in front of you and appreciate the moment you are in.

April 29

THERE IS A TREASURE TROVE OF JOY to be found in
each day. Today is a puzzle and the clues for happiness
are all around. Look for the good in each interaction and
place you encounter. Redirect your thoughts when you feel
yourself drawn to negativity. If we search for the positive,
our minds are calibrated to find it. Be open to discovery, like
an explorer on an open sea. The excitement of searching is
half the fun.

April 30

DETERMINATION CAN CREATE A LIFE of ease if we
work hard and plan well. To find your flow, it's important to
find a balance between work and rest. The elusive arrival
of balance can create anxiety in our lives. But if we are
determined, work hard, and honor the blessings we are given,
a sense of ease arrives. Be thankful for the work you do, the
abundance you have, and the life you are creating. You are
creating your destiny.

May 1

IN THE BEGINNING OF SOMETHING NEW, we feel excitement. It brings our awareness to possibility, hope, and even creativity. When we begin, anything is possible. The shape of something new is limitless. Every morning we have the opportunity to see the day this way. We can choose to see the hope of beginning and allow our creativity to shape the day we desire. When we choose creativity over comfort, our day becomes brighter and more exciting. How can you be creative today?

May 2

AS A FLOWER OPENS ITS PETALS to greet the sun, it reveals what was once held tight in a bud. All the intricacies of the flower are open for all to see, and it is beautiful, delicate, and complex. The flower is not worried about anything other than greeting a new day and soaking up the lovely rays of sunshine. In order to receive light, we must be open to it. We must relax our grasp and open so that light can enter every part of us, especially the places that need it most.

May 3

WHEN YOU FEEL YOURSELF caught in a trap of comparing yourself to others, take a moment to breathe and connect with your heart. There is no one else like you. Everyone is on their own journey and it's not fair to compare yourself to their distinctive path. Remind yourself of where you want to be headed and move toward your objectives. By keeping your eyes on your goals, the perception of what others are doing will become less important.

May 4

RIGHT BEFORE A FLOWER BLOOMS, a gardener waits with anticipation. She grew the plant from a seed, tended the soil, and watered it to reach this point. A bloom reflects the plant's health. It's exciting to wait for things that you've worked hard for. What is about to blossom in your life? Take a moment to reflect on the moves you've made to get here with pride and appreciation. Your efforts are to be celebrated!

May 5

THE CHANGES THAT OCCUR in life are sometimes designed to uproot you, challenge you, and make you question whether your strength is being tested. These times are difficult, and it can feel as if there is no end in sight. But this season will end. All things come to an end. Know this: You are stronger than you give yourself credit for. You can handle hard things. When you get through this, your strength will have increased and your spirit will be more resilient. You can do this!

May 6

WHEN ACTION STEMS FROM REACTION, we are rooted in hurt. It's easy to react from a place of aching. When our feelings get hurt, we want to protect ourselves. But if we allow the painful feelings to dissipate, we can respond with a calmer mind and heart. From here, healing can begin. If we accept and forgive, we will experience transformation. Acting from a place of calm can diffuse tense situations. Remember your breath and move forward with love.

May 7

A FEATHER FLOATS THROUGH the sky, not knowing which direction it will take. As it drifts along with the wind, it looks free. Freedom is supposed to feel airy and happy. If you are feeling free, embrace the feeling. Reject the feeling of guilt and enjoy the ride. Once you set a boundary or make a decision to be free, smile and breathe in the space you've created. Don't apologize for creating space in your life. Embrace the freedom you've created with gratitude.

———

May 8

YOU MAY NOT WANT TO wake up this morning to do what you need to do. It may feel better to stay in bed. But after you tap the snooze button a few times, encourage and motivate yourself to get up and move. You'll feel better and ready to tackle the day with a clear head. Next time you feel like sleeping in, think about a way to take on the day and do it. Wake up! Life is waiting for you to partake in!

May 9

A ROSE BLOOMS IN A PATTERN of perfection. Each petal has a place and unfolds with perfect timing. As the blossom unfurls, it releases an intoxicating scent. The scent of the rose carries the highest vibrational scent and elevates the mood of those who stop to smell it. If you pass by a rosebush today, stop. Take the time to infuse your day with high vibrations just by smelling a flower. This mindful act will elevate your mood and add positivity to your day.

May 10

DEALING WITH ADVERSITY is never pleasant but gives us an opportunity to grow and find a deeper understanding of others. Remember to breathe when hardship finds you and take time to process your thoughts. Then reframe negative thoughts or judgments. In difficult times, we often need compassion for healing to occur. Reframe, forgive, and let go. See the lesson and not the struggle. You will get through this stronger and wiser.

May 11

NEGATIVE THOUGHTS AND EMOTIONS can be addictive, yet they hold us back. Are some of your thought patterns holding you back? Retrain your brain to think positively. When a negative thought comes up, recognize it, stop the thought, and replace it with a positive one. The more you practice, the easier it is to rework negativity. Try this daily and notice how your thoughts change from negative to more positive.

———

May 12

SAILORS AT SEA KNOW they are close to land when they see sparrows flying above. After a long journey, it is comforting to know that home is near. Each passing wave brings the ship closer to land. The sailors offer a prayer for a safe journey. It feels good to return home. Set yourself up for success by leaving your home ready to receive you. Each day provides a journey, so create a space you want to return to.

May 13

YOU ARE A VIBRANT and brilliant soul. You have the gift of insight and are exceptional at making things happen. Light emanates from your core, illuminating all who come in contact with you. Like the sun, you bring a generous warmth. Your soul has power and your purpose lies deep within you. Bring your stunning colors to all you encounter today. The world needs your unique beauty and vivacious heart. We are lucky to have you in this world.

May 14

FREEDOM COMES THROUGH FORGIVENESS. When we hold on to hurt, our hearts and minds fill with negativity, which slowly eats away at our spirit. Forgive those who hurt you and release any pain, resentment, or bitterness that has taken root. Allow freedom to pass through you. Let go of the need to control the outcome and people's reactions. Don't continue to suffer long after the pain occurred. Choose to forgive over and over so that freedom and love can return.

May 15

AS THE WIND SWEEPS ACROSS the plains, the grass dances in response. Like an ocean wave, the grass rises and falls with the force of the wind. It's mesmerizing and lovely to watch. Even a flat landscape has its own peculiar charm, with golden grass swaying and a bigger-than-life blue sky above. No matter where you find yourself today, be like the grass and sway in the wind instead of resisting what is.

———

May 16

MORNING ROUTINES ARE vital to our success. When we take time each morning to ground ourselves, we set the tone for our day. Take at least ten minutes every morning to quiet your mind, reflect, and offer gratitude: you're likelier to feel at peace and geared for success. Find some time to sit quietly this morning; you can do this anywhere. Breathe in gratitude for the moments of stillness and for the day ahead.

May 17

SEND LOVE OUT TO THE PEOPLE in your life every day: this is a beautiful way to begin your day. By focusing your attention on someone else and holding them in your heart with love; you create an energetic effect that can be felt from afar. This can be especially helpful if someone you know is experiencing a difficult time. Send them love; feel the love you have for them in your core, and then send it their way.

May 18

A ROOSTER CROWS SIGNALING the start of a new day. Soon after his morning call, the sun surfaces over the horizon. Every day, he knows when dawn is going to break because of his internal clock. Through instinct, he acts. Our internal clock and biological instincts provide us with important cues, like waking up each day. Think about the things your body just knows it needs to do. Our bodies are amazing and deserve love and appreciation each day.

May 19

EVERY MORNING PROVIDES an opportunity for expansion. After you sleep, stretch your body to activate a flow of energy. Take deep breaths to awaken your organs and mind. Visualize your day from the highest perspective, creating a soulful blueprint. Expand your awareness and be open to the unknown, letting go of any expectations or fears. Choose to grow today. Life is meant to be full of progress. How will you choose to expand?

May 20

LIFE CAN FEEL HECTIC. Our lists continue to grow. We take on more than we can handle, and then stress and fatigue set in. When you feel overwhelmed and pulled in several directions, take the time to be here now. Reset your busy mind. To provide your soul a moment of solace, relinquish the need to be busy and just be still. Take deep breaths and remember that nothing is more important than the breaths you take.

May 21

WE WILL ALWAYS HAVE room for improvement—and trying to reach perfection will only cause us to live in a furnace of anxiety. The only thing we can do is try our best and allow ourselves to learn and grow from our mistakes. Perfection is an illusion. Think about all the effort you put into trying to be perfect. Abandon the intoxicating lure of perfection. Life is full of lessons and there is great beauty in imperfection.

May 22

WHEN WE GO THROUGH A VALLEY, it can seem like everything around us is overwhelming and towering over our heads. We may feel as if things are impossible and that we are at the bottom, with impossible heights to climb. And yet, the valley has the most fertile ground; it's here that growth happens and strength is renewed. Rivers glide through the valley and plants thrive. Be like the river and know that you have the strength to reach the summit of the mountain.

May 23

OUR HEARTS SPEAK VOLUMES. We can learn and grow from intuitive clues if we know how to listen in stillness. Intuition gives signs as to how we can fulfill our desires and take the necessary actions to make our dreams come true. To find your intuition, take some time to sit in silence. While sitting in silence, listen to what your heart has to say. It may take practice, but in time you will recognize your inner voice.

May 24

TIME IS A GIFT and we can often go through life feeling as if we don't have enough of it. When we believe this, it is based in fear and scarcity. Notice any activities that take over your day. Refocus your attention and do one thing at a time. When we scatter our attention, the illusion of time distorts. We have exactly the amount of hours we need.

May 25

RISE LIKE THE SUN: awaken each part of your body gently, intentionally, and slowly. Feel your breath fill your lungs, sending oxygen to your extremities. Let your senses come alive, sending energetic vibrations throughout your body. Take in the sights and sounds of the morning with deep awareness. Take your time as you move through your morning. Greet the day from a place of gentleness as you gradually develop a routine.

May 26

BEGIN THE DAY WITH these powerful affirmations: *I am more powerful than I give myself credit for. Everything I have been through has prepared me for where I am headed. I have overcome great trials and pain. My life is a beautiful tapestry of triumph. I harness my inner courage to conquer the next obstacle life has in store, because it will only make me stronger. I am capable of great things and refuse to play small. Today I step forward with bravery and strength.*

May 27

SOMETIMES WHAT WE THINK we want isn't what we need—and the pursuit of it causes us resistance and anxiety. When you find yourself in the midst of this type of confusion, take some time to center yourself and find your intuition: your deep inner well of wisdom. Surrender to what is meant to be and let go of whatever you are holding on to. Answers arrive when we let go and make room for what's meant to enter our lives.

———

May 28

BEFORE YOU GET OUT OF BED, take a moment to notice everything around you. What do you hear? What do you feel? What do you see? Scan your body and recognize any places that feel great. Send gratitude to those places. If there are any areas that feel off, acknowledge them and send them love. Breathe in the abundant oxygen and smile. Today is a new day and you are about to enter it with a new level of awareness. May you be present and aware throughout the day.

May 29

AS THE TIDES CHANGE, taking parts of the Earth with them, the ocean remains the same. The ocean is a powerful force, able to wear down cliffs into sand. Its power is magnificent. It is humbling to stand on the shore of such a mighty force. It is powerful to comprehend that out past the horizon, the ocean continues for thousands of miles. The ocean reminds us that nothing is permanent and all things eventually wash away.

May 30

EVERY MORNING WE HAVE the opportunity to choose joy! Choose to be happy in this moment. Think about something that brings you joy and feel it deep within. Feel yourself well up with happiness as you think about this joyful memory or promising future. Take this feeling and know that you can connect to it all day. You have the power to change your mind—and that is such an amazing thing!

May 31

TRUE VIBRANCY COMES FROM WITHIN. The light in our eyes, the radiance in a smile, the glow of our skin are all manifestations of how we take care of ourselves inwardly. Spiritual health is just as important as physical health. Take some time each day to find your light. Breathe in your brilliance, breathe out the chaos. When we access our light, we can feel our inner power expand. When you glow from within, you are magnetic.

June 1

THE MORNING BRINGS a clean slate for you to write your story. How do you want the day to go? You have the power to make today feel the way you want. Even when things seem off, you can still choose to feel how you desire. Take a moment and find the tone you want to set for the day. Now take a deep breath and really *feel* this feeling. You have the power to tap into that all day long.

June 2

WE ARE ALWAYS SEEKING balance in our lives. It feels like an endless quest to try to divide our time equally among all the parts of our lives in perfect harmony. But this is not the reality for most people—and perhaps balance means our time is allocated differently as needs arise. The need for perfect balance can be stressful. What if your life is exactly as it needs to be in this moment? Peace comes from accepting what is.

———

June 3

WE ALL WANT TO BELONG and feel accepted. There is a spark inside you that makes you unique. People are lucky to know you. Take down the walls you've built to protect your heart. If you've been hurt before, release the pain of those memories and do the work to mend the place where the wound began. Not everyone is supposed to stay in our lives, but the ones who stay are worthy of our hearts. Open your heart to those people. Love and acceptance are on the other side of the wall.

June 4

WHEN A CAT WAKES UP, it does so at a leisurely pace. It takes the time to stretch its limbs and curl its back. A cat is not in a hurry to wake up and do anything. It revels in the rest it just awoke from. Practice getting up slowly, stretching each limb. Feel yourself gradually awaken as you send movement through your body. The rest you just had was much needed. Take your time to transition from it.

June 5

LIFE IS TRULY AMAZING! Just think about all you've gone through to get where you are right now. You've had many milestones and made several decisions to get here. You have accomplished so many things and have made an impact on various lives. Even the things that felt like mistakes brought you to this moment, which is exactly where you're meant to be. You have a full day ahead of you. How will you add to the story of your life?

June 6

YOU KNOW THAT MOMENT when you realize that everything has lined up perfectly, perhaps serendipitously? It's remarkable and you should celebrate these moments. Serendipity feels like a big hug from the universe. It results in exclamations like "I can't believe this happened!" and "It was perfect timing!" When life presents itself this way, celebrate with gratitude and reverence. Things line up when they are supposed to. Timing is everything and when it's least expected, it's the most exciting.

———

June 7

BE GENTLE WITH YOURSELF TODAY. Take the day to notice your body's cues. Listen to your intuition. Slow down. There is no need to rush through this day, mindlessly producing. When we get wrapped up in this mindset, we tend to ignore the subtle signs our bodies send out. Take time today to stop and listen to your intuitive cues. Learn the messages so that when they present themselves you will recognize them and heed to your needs. With gentleness, great healing can happen.

June 8

IN A GARDEN, food grows from a tiny seed. Some plants make their way to the surface and grow in plain sight, while others stay underground, showcasing only their greenery. No matter where they grow, they offer nutrition and sustenance. Sometimes our personal growth is outward for all to see and other times it is hidden from sight. You are always growing. Even when there isn't physical evidence, growth is inevitable.

June 9

EVERYONE HAS A PURPOSE. You are here for a reason. When it doesn't seem clear to you, reflect on the things that spark you up inside and the things you do well. Our purpose isn't necessarily what we do for work. Our purpose is the reason our souls are on Earth. By taking the time to discover your purpose, you will help create fulfillment in your life because your soul will feel at peace.

June 10

WHAT DO YOU WANT to accomplish today? There is
a full day ahead with a fresh canvas for you to paint a
beautiful picture. What will it look like at the end of the day?
Consider what needs to get done and sprinkle in something
nonessential and memorable. Our days aren't supposed to
be a list of tasks. Each day is a blessing and it's up to you
to make it lovely.

———

June 11

WE CARRY STORIES OF the generations before us.
Our families pass down their hopes, dreams, and fears
to the next generation. If you come from a family whose
messages were broken and painful, you have the power to
break those patterns. It's not our responsibility to carry those
wounds. It's okay to release their grasp and write a new
narrative from your level of understanding. With the right help
and time, you can forgive and heal these familial wounds.

June 12

A BIRD BUILDS A NEST to prepare for new life. It spends time finding pieces to create a safe place for its eggs to hatch. A lot of planning goes into preparing for new life. The nest is a symbol of home and protection—a place for growth. For a short period, the chicks are fed and protected and then they listen to instinct and fly. Listen to your instinct and in time take flight. You may soar, but first you must jump.

June 13

EVERYTHING WORKS OUT in its own time. Although that may seem impossible, whatever you are facing will resolve. A release comes with surrender. The parts of you that felt tense trying to control and hold on become loose and open when you let go. Thoughts go from fear to trust and your heart calms down. Practice trusting and releasing. Contracting only deflects what's meant to be. Expand in trust and open your arms to receive.

June 14

FRIENDSHIP IS A GIFT. The people in your life are there because you have taken the time to cultivate a reciprocal relationship. When we open our hearts to another, we create a space where love can blossom. Take a moment to think about your friendships and give thanks for each person who has offered you that gift. Let your friends know how much they mean to you today. Affirm their existence in your heart and keep the love alive.

June 15

CHOOSE THE ADVENTURE your life provides. Each day is a blank page, ready to be filled with our ups and downs, which create a beautiful story. Even though the adventure is not always easy, vibrancy comes through resilience, overcoming, and the happiness that awaits us on the other side of every trial. Each adventure presents itself as a way to recalibrate our light more brilliantly.

June 16

SOMETIMES WE ARE INCLINED to go through all the things that could happen and go wrong. These thought spirals send out negative energy, creating anxiety and tension in our bodies. When you find yourself full of anxiety, place your attention on the present moment. When we zero in on what could go wrong, we form scenarios that may never happen. Interrupt the pattern by infusing your thoughts with positive energy, which will attract positive energy and alleviate anxious thoughts.

June 17

TODAY IS THE PERFECT DAY to create the change you desire. Life is too short to dwell in misery, hoping that someday things will change. You could make a million excuses as to why right now isn't the right time, but then you will never find the perfect time to do anything. Perfection is an illusion. If we keep waiting for the stars to align, we will reach the end of our lives regretting that we never tried. Stop the waiting game and take action toward the change you want.

June 18

THEY ARE WILD AND FREE, the ones who embrace life with joy. They are peaceful and serene, the ones who find time to be quiet and still. They are joyful and creative, the ones who open their minds to possibility and growth. You too can be all of these things! Find time for quiet and see the world as full of possibility. Embrace all that comes your way.

———

June 19

YOU HAVE THE POWER to imagine how you want your life to look. Our thoughts are quite powerful and can create our reality. Where our focus goes, energy flows. If you want something to change, focus on the outcome you want and not what isn't working. Spend your energy on the solution, not the problem. Envision the way you would like to feel. Change your reality by visualizing and then moving toward where you want to go.

June 20

FOR FRUIT TO GROW, the soil needs to be fertile and water plentiful. During the growth and ripening season, we pull weeds that hinder growth. Roots grow deeper as the plant grows to support the weight of the fruit. In our own lives, we can also pull weeds to allow beautiful things to ripen. Unless growth is the focal point, we can easily become sidetracked by things that keep us from reaching our potential. By staying focused, we become more grounded in our purpose.

June 21

EACH OF US HAS A TALENT to share with the world. We are born with these talents or develop them, and they burn like a fire inside our souls. We are all creative in our own way. It takes courage to create and share something that comes from the soul—and your skill is best when shared. You never know who may need to receive your talent. Sometimes all we need is an audience of one. Create without expectation. Let the fire within you bring passion and light into the world.

June 22

WHEN WE SPEND TIME IN OUR HEADS, it takes away from experiencing life at its fullest. We may end up spending more time interpreting than experiencing. Overthinking can kill creativity and inspiration. Allow things not to make sense. Sometimes the present moment doesn't need a meaning. Not everything needs to make sense immediately. Welcome ambiguity and let things unfold in their own time. Give your intuition room to speak and your mind room to rest. Release the need to know and just be here, right now.

June 23

EVERYTHING IS CONNECTED. We are all part of the same universal energy, and the way we interpret experiences is a direct correlation to how we experience life. What we see and feel reflects who we are inside. What we focus on expands. Choose to expand in love, forgiveness, and grace. See and honor the goodness and beauty in each soul and thing you encounter today, and their goodness and beauty will flicker through.

June 24

DECIDE TO LET GO TODAY and repeat the following:
*I choose to let go of pain and forgive the resentments I am
holding on to. I am releasing the grip of control I desire in
this situation and open my heart to healing. I am sending
love to those who have hurt me, and I allow my heart to
relax. My healing is a journey and I welcome the lessons
this situation has presented. My wounds catapult me into
deeper understanding and empathy. I am grateful for
these lessons.*

June 25

IT'S HARDER TO SHINE on some days than on others.
No matter what we do, we just can't seem to make things
happen. This is when we need rest. Permit yourself to
pause when things aren't working out. When you stop
trying and striving, your body and mind can receive the gift
of rest and restoration. Be gracious with yourself and listen
to what your body needs.

June 26

IN THE MIDDLE OF A MEADOW, a deer grazes peacefully. The songs of birds fill the trees. Out in the distance, the mountaintops are still covered in snow. Everything is serene and the breeze gently blows through. When you take time to be mindful, your mind can be like this meadow scene. When there is chaos streaming through your mind, you can stop, reflect on a tranquil scene, and just breathe. In that moment, you don't need to complete anything but your next breath.

June 27

INVITE THE SACRED INTO EACH DAY. Whether it's a prayer, moments of meditation, or enjoying nature's enchantment, choose to find something greater than you and surrender to its grandeur. Tapping into the sacred invites harmony, curiosity, and wisdom into your life. When you feel insignificant, remember that your soul is here for a purpose. When you feel alone, remember that you are part of something greater than yourself. When you feel discouraged, remind yourself of how far you've come.

June 28

EVERYTHING IN NATURE has something to offer.
A flower offers pollen to the birds and bees. The sun offers
luminosity and warmth. The snow offers water to rivers as
it melts. The rain offers relief to the parched Earth. What is
your offering? Think about how you serve others and show
up each day. If you aren't using your talents, find a way to
implement them into your life. Walk into your strength and
own your power. Your offering is your present to the world.

———

June 29

START SOMETHING NEW, especially when you feel stuck.
Inviting newness into your life brings joy and creativity.
Take a new route to work, try a different food or get going
on a new project you've been thinking about starting.
Create momentum in your life to invite and embrace change.
Change can be scary, but also rewarding. When we start
something new, we expand our minds and horizons.
Be open and fluid. Trust that what is meant to enter
your life will come.

June 30

IT'S DIFFICULT WHEN things don't go the way we
planned. When we get caught up in our expectations,
we leave little room for change to take place. Be flexible.
Accept things as they appear. Everything is happening
as it should and in perfect timing. Once you can release
the expectation and be open to what is, you will find
acceptance. Notice how everything is working together and
know that although all of the answers may not be apparent
now, in time they will be.

July 1

WALKING THROUGH A REDWOOD FOREST, your footsteps are muted by a bed of pine needles on the forest floor. The towering trees offer a reverent sense of silence. As they reach up to the heavens, they create a natural cathedral, a space to find the sacred. The soul knows what it needs when it's in the presence of nature. Find a place in nature today where you can tap into your soul and create a sacred moment, wherever you may be. Invite the healing power of nature into your day.

July 2

A GOAL MAY FEEL AS IF you have a mountain to climb, but great things are done in steps. If you really want something, break it down into action steps. Ask yourself, "What is one thing I can do today to get closer to my goal?" And then ask that question again tomorrow. Before you know it, you're halfway up the mountain. Remember that every step is worthy of gratitude and awe.

July 3

AS THE SUN WARMS THE GROUND, the flowers open and birds fly around, looking for food. Morning is a time of preparation and opening. It's a lovely time to prepare for the day and visualize the outcomes you desire. What do you need to prepare for today? What is opening in your life? Today is the perfect day to work toward your dreams and open up to possibilities. When we take the time to prepare, our days transpire more effectively.

July 4

THE PEACEFULNESS OF A QUIET morning can continue throughout the day. We wake up from a dream state with a fresh mind. Too often we allow daily stresses and anxieties to quickly take over, robbing us of the peace we woke up with. When stress takes over, we give away our power to whatever caused the stress. When we allow anxiety to take over, we give our power away to the unknown. Invite peace and the unknown in.

July 5

IN A FOREST, all forms of life support one another. The soil provides nutrients for the plants and trees, which provide shade, oxygen, and food for the animals. Even the animals provide important nutrients and help control overgrowth. Everything works in a precious equilibrium. Nature intuitively knows what it needs to thrive, just as your intuition knows what you need. Spend some time in silence this morning to tap into your inner wisdom. Everything you need is within; create space for the answers to be revealed.

July 6

SOME THINGS TAKE LONGER than others. The end goal may not be the reward; perhaps the process is. We can learn many lessons along the way. Growth, insight, and perseverance are some of the results we can see throughout the process. If something is taking longer than expected, stop and reflect on what you stand to gain during the wait. Be patient and thankful, even if it seems tough. Transitions generate discomfort and help us achieve a new level of comfort.

July 7

SPEAK TO YOURSELF as you would to the one you love the most. Honor and respect your mind, body, and soul. Take care of yourself by catching negative self-talk and reframing self-judgments. You deserve kindness, love, and approval. Say something loving to yourself each morning. With practice, your thoughts toward yourself and others will change. Love will emit from you powerfully and you will become irresistible.

———

July 8

EARLY ON A SUMMER MORNING, the air may have a slight chill. It feels crisp and refreshing right before the heat sets in. As the Earth warms up, flowers open to face the rising sun and the water sparkles with the sun's reflection. Then as night falls, the cooling begins and the cycle continues. Everything is cyclical. Nothing is permanent. If you are feeling stressed about something, know that it will pass. Breathe in strength; you will get through this.

July 9

A SUNRISE TAKES ITS TIME. The sun is in no rush to reveal itself. It slowly creeps over the horizon, illuminating what was once dark. As it rises, it changes the sky from deep midnight blue to soft pink and orange—a remarkable sight to behold. If you are waiting for something to appear, know that good things take time. Take in the allure of the sunrise. It appears for only a moment and the most stunning moment is sometimes right before it emerges.

———

July 10

A HONEYBEE FLIES from flower to flower looking for sweet nectar to create honey. The bee works to find the flowers with the sweetest nectar and doesn't stop until it finds what it's looking for. Don't stop searching for what you're looking for either. Persevere and know that something amazing could be waiting just around the corner. The anticipatory excitement of a journey makes life extraordinary. Soon you will find what you need and be able to revel in the journey.

July 11

HEALING COMES IN WAVES. Sometimes we feel as if we're drowning in sorrow. At other times it feels as if we are riding a wave without a care in the world. Don't rush your heart to heal. Allow the swells to come. When calm finally arrives, bless the pain and the lessons it brought. In time you will feel better, stronger, and more resilient. This time is a gift. Let your heart express all the feelings that come. You are making room for what's *meant* to come.

———

July 12

IF THERE IS SOMETHING you want to do or create, start today. You don't have to be completely ready. Action will set everything in motion, and even if you don't know where to begin or don't feel prepared, start before you're ready knowing that everything will fall into place as it needs to. Quit making excuses and just act. To get started, think of one thing you can do today and do it. Your future will thank you for it.

July 13

EACH OF OUR FRIENDS were once strangers. Think about each person in your life who has made a difference. These people were once unknown and eventually, you created a bond of trust and love with each of them. Every person we meet has the possibility to impact our lives in a positive way. Treat each stranger with love and respect as you never know where an interaction may lead. Keep your heart and mind open to the possibilities.

July 14

DEEP IN THE TREES, cicadas play a buzzing symphony. Their songs carry and each tree's colony responds with its own chorus. The buzzing noise is electric as the cicadas signal that they are alive. They sing their song only after years of hibernation. They are alive and letting everyone know it. Think about how amazing it is to be alive and the power each breath brings. Play your own symphony. Use your voice and talents. Share your electricity with others and encourage them to share theirs with you.

July 15

AS YOU START YOUR MORNING, repeat the following words to yourself: *I choose to be content with what I have. Everything I need is available to me. I am grateful for the sleep I had last night and for this gorgeous morning, full of possibility. I look forward to this day with hope and am inspired to see the good in everyone I meet. Today is the perfect day to take a step in the life I desire. My future is bright because I am making a difference.*

July 16

THE WARMTH OF THE SUMMER sun permeates everything it encounters. It creates energy and growth. The days are longer as the sun lingers, glistening deep into the evening. When you express warmth and emit energy, you leave a lasting impression with everyone you encounter. Your energy speaks volumes. Think about a time when someone left a lasting impression on you. How did it make you feel? People remember the way you make them feel. How do you want to leave your mark?

July 17

WHEN THINGS ARE UNCOMFORTABLE, it's easy to give up and walk away. If we never push past our discomfort, we will never find the understanding and wisdom that awaits us on the other side. Discomfort is a gift. It brings a deeper meaning to life. The growth that occurs after a period of difficulty leads to resilience and empathy. Choose to see discomfort as a gift to help others and not as a burden. We become polished through pressure, not ease.

July 18

EVERY DAY WE HAVE THE CHANCE to ascend like the sun and share our light. Even on foggy mornings, the sun finds its way through, if only to offer its light dimly. No matter what the conditions are, the sun still glimmers. If you are feeling less vibrant than usual today, take a moment to locate your inner power. Breathe into this powerful space that is within you. It is always available to help you rise up.

July 19

WAKE UP AND SEIZE THE DAY. A beautiful world with amazing people is just waiting to be explored. Breathe in the crisp morning air, fill your lungs with the abundant oxygen available, and offer gratitude for the opportunity to be alive right here, right now. You can make today whatever you want it to be. You have the power to create your reality. How will you seize this day and add beauty to your surroundings?

July 20

THERE IS HELP ALL AROUND. If you are feeling overwhelmed, you don't have to go through it alone. Reach out for help. Let someone know how you are feeling. If you know someone who is in pain, be there for them. Reach out to your friends and family and check in, even if they seem okay. We are built for connection, not isolation. Build a bridge of compassion and if you need that bridge to come to you, ask for help.

July 21

IT TAKES COURAGE to show tenderness. Expressing our feelings and offering empathy is an act of soulful bravery. When we can let our guard down to share our heart and offer it to others, we risk being rejected or misunderstood. But there is a greater reward when our tenderness brings healing to a relationship, comfort to another, and ease to our bodies. Courage comes from living with openness. When we soften, we allow love to take root and open our hearts.

July 22

YOU HAVE A TREASURE trove of wisdom within. All that you have experienced, learned, and created has cultivated an inner guide for your soul. You are here on your own journey, and it is full of wonder if you open your eyes to see all that life has to offer. Accept the adventure of being alive. Embrace the deep well of wisdom your soul has accumulated. Your soul is the compass for your adventure and your wisdom is the testament of your life.

July 23

STRESS AND ANXIETY CREATE blocks in our lives. Flow creates peace and harmony. When we struggle with what's happening, we move out of flow. Everything is happening exactly as it should. Trust that your efforts and prayers are being recognized. Do your best and create change. Life will unfold as it does. We are responsible for how we react and the choices we make as it does. Trust and faith can eliminate anxiety and stress. We are given a wonderful life to live and experience.

July 24

A TREE GROWS TO REACH for the sun. As it grows, branches and leaves develop to feed on the nourishing rays of the sun. No matter how tall the tree becomes, it remains grounded in the Earth with roots growing deeper and wider to support it. We can always reach higher and remain grounded at the same time. As you reach for your aspirations, remember to stay grounded as you grow. Be like a tree and stay humble as you ascend.

July 25

BALMY SUMMER MORNINGS remind us to take things a little slower and revel in the season of play. Summer lasts for only a short time. This is the time when the sun lingers in the sky. Take a cue from the sun by taking your time. Feeling rushed robs us of experiencing the moment. If you are feeling overwhelmed, notice any unnecessary tasks that steal your time. Take the time to really experience what matters and let go of the rest.

July 26

FREEDOM COMES FROM THE TRUTH, but the truth is not always easy to speak or even live. Our truth can be uncomfortable for others, but if not expressed can cause us the greatest discomfort. When we live in our truth, we feel lighter and free. Even if admitting the truth is tough, the weight lifted from speaking it is worth our effort. What is something you need to express? How can you acknowledge your truth? Choose freedom over comfort.

July 27

HELPING OTHERS IS A GIFT, and when you see the opportunity to be of service you enrich someone's life by helping. You may find great joy in giving of yourself in service but make sure there is a balance to your giving. Don't give to the point of exhaustion. Take moments to recharge. You too deserve help and support. Be mindful of your limits and give yourself the gift of rest. Fill your cup so you can continue to give with love.

July 28

IT'S A MYSTERY HOW WE end up in the families that we do. If you had a difficult childhood, forgiveness and healing are available with time. Your wounds can be a light for others in similar situations. Healing takes strength and your soul knows its capabilities. Some of the strongest souls heal from harsh realities. You are a miracle and your survival is proof of your strength and resilience.

July 29

IF YOUR LIFE IS NOT GOING the way you'd like it to, you have the power to change it. Sometimes it may seem impossible to produce the change you desire. As you choose your own path every day, be clear about what it is you truly want. Each day, you can move closer to the life you want with intention and focus. Welcome all the wonderful things life has to offer. Take control and decide to focus on what you want and not on what isn't working.

July 30

WHEN WE TAKE THINGS too seriously we leave little room for play and excitement. Life is intended to be enjoyed and we have many opportunities to be spontaneous and bring awe into our lives. Look around and take delight in the smallest things. Let your mind wander into the joy of simple pleasures. Laugh at yourself and with others. Let go of the need to be perfect. Hold loosely to ideals and leave room for curiosity to take over.

July 31

ENDINGS CREATE SPACE FOR REBIRTH. Things must end to allow what is meant to be to happen. What is longing to grow in your life? Is there anything you are holding on to that is preventing that growth? Let go of your attachment to people and things that no longer serve you. Attachment only creates pain, especially when we need to release what we are holding on to. Wait patiently for rebirth to take place. Transformations are beautiful.

August 1

EARLY ON A SUMMER MORNING, the lake is still. Before any boats are out, the water is like a mirror, reflecting the sky above. Birds glide peacefully, leaving ripples behind them. The sun slowly rises, creating sparkles across the water. Everything has a moment to awaken in its own timing. Mornings offer stillness before anything needs to happen. Be like a lake and reflect before you move. In these moments you can awaken at your own pace.

August 2

ACKNOWLEDGE YOUR RESILIENCE and wisdom, given all the times you got back up after a loss or a failure. It's hard to generate momentum after things go wrong. The ability to start again, walk away, and most of all forgive, strengthens our hearts and will to survive. If you feel as if things aren't falling into place, let go and know that your spirit is strong. What is planned for you is on its way.

August 3

THE MORNING OFFERS COOLNESS before the temperatures increase. An energy of excitement coincides with a new day because so many things are possible. Choose the center of your interests today and prioritize your tasks. As things come in, put them aside until the project at hand is complete. You are making things happen, and you will accomplish everything that is important.

———

August 4

OUR ENERGY CAN BE WRAPPED up in another person, blocking the flow of life. If this person is no longer in your life, release them. Allow the life force of freedom to pass through you by letting go of residual energetic ties. Send the person love as you redirect your energy to those who show up for you. Take back your power by reclaiming what you gave away. Your presence is a gift; give it wisely.

August 5

EVERY MORNING, IT'S IMPORTANT to spend time in solitude to hear your soul speak. We can hear the stirrings of our soul in silence and with presence. When we spend our first moments in solitude, the day feels more peaceful. In this space you can decide without distraction how you want to enter the day. By choosing to check in with yourself first thing—instead of reaching for information—you're choosing to create your reality before taking in the reality of others.

————

August 6

SOMETIMES LIFE IS REALLY HARD. It can feel as if challenges persist—and yet, strength comes from challenges. The things we wish weren't happening are actually creating resilience and a new level of wisdom. You are transforming under pressure. When we open our souls to new lessons, growth takes place. You will become an inspiration to others and your light will radiate on the other side of the tears and pain. Welcome the challenge and empower yourself to transform.

August 7

TRYING TO MAKE SOMETHING work that isn't designed to work gives us a sense of false control. We can't make people and situations bend to our will. As much as we want something to work, sometimes things just need to fall away. Knowing when to let go and when to hang on is a great lesson. If you are met with resistance, it's time to change your approach or move on. Through the struggle a new sense of ease and comfort will emerge.

August 8

HOLDING SPACE FOR ANOTHER PERSON requires active listening through presence and respect. When people share their stories, they are inviting you in with a bid for connection. Giving them the time and space to express themselves is an offering and deep connections are formed with each interaction. We tend to get wrapped up in our own story when we need to listen. Try to really hear what they are saying and offer the empathy and love they are seeking. Open your ears when others choose you to open their hearts to you.

August 9

FIERCE DETERMINATION CAN bring many wonderful things into our lives. It takes hard work and focus to create greatness. When we put our minds toward what we want instead of what isn't working, we harness our potential to make things happen. Think about your deepest desires and make a move toward those desires today. Keep going until you are closer to your desired outcome. You have the power to be the change you want to see.

—————

August 10

EARLY MORNING LIGHT APPEARS on the horizon, painting the sky with cool hues of pink, lavender, and yellow. Right before everything is illuminated, the sky looks like a watercolor painting. As the sun continues to emanate, the cool hues change into a warm glow, illuminating everything with golden light. We too can, like the sun, steadily turn up our radiance. Allow time for slowness in the morning to calibrate your inner glow. Be like the sun and let your warmth emanate.

August 11

EVERY DAY IS AN OPPORTUNITY to make a difference. As we go through our days, we can be aware of the needs around us. When we start doing for others, our hearts change. We can make a difference in so many ways through actions, words, and thoughts. The power of our intention transforms our energy, which in turn affects everyone around us. If our eyes are open to the needs of others, we can become part of a catalyst for change.

———

August 12

IT TAKES A BOLD SPIRIT to go after what you really want. When we know we need to make a change, fear of the unknown can keep us from expanding our horizons. You are brave. There are things that you have done that you weren't ready for and somehow, here you are, stronger and ready to take the next leap. What is something that you want to do? Identify what's holding you back and move into your power by taking a step toward your dreams and away from fear.

August 13

A WATERFALL SURGES when the rain provides water to rivers. As the seasons change, its power slows to a trickle and sometimes dries up. Even when a waterfall isn't surging, its effects are apparent by the erosion on the rock's face. Creativity is like a waterfall: it comes and goes, but its effects change the creator. Every act of creativity leaves its mark. Just as the rain replenishes rivers, creativity returns to pour out of the creator. How will you create today?

August 14

CHOOSING JOY WHEN LIFE feels heavy can be a potent shift in perspective and energy. Take the time to quiet discontent, sadness, frustration, and anxiety with joy to interrupt the comfort we feel in lower emotional states. When we flood our bodies with memories of purely joyful moments, we change our chemistry and the way we react. Our nervous system responds to the flood of positive emotions and our mood lifts. Think about a time when you felt immense joy. Carry that moment with you throughout the day.

August 15

WHAT IS YOUR SUPERPOWER? There are many things that we are good at and our superpower is the one thing that if we didn't do it, we would feel a void in our life. This is the thing that you're passionate about; that people come to you for. Tap into your inner power and find the things that keep you from sharing your talents. Do less of what drains your power and more of what empowers you.

———

August 16

DOWN BY THE OCEAN, the marine layer envelopes the sky, shielding the sun's gleam. Mornings stay cool with this blanket of clouds before the sun's heat burns it off to shine through. The gray sky has a beautiful stillness and provides protection from the sun's heat. Movement is easier under the coolness of the marine layer and thoughts seems to blossom before the day becomes bright under the sun. It's the perfect time for reflection and action.

August 17

GRATITUDE RELEASES THE HOLD that discontentment may have on us. When we make a habit of noticing the things we are thankful for, our minds begin to look for such things. The more we practice gratitude, the easier it is to see the good in each day. What didn't seem like enough now seems like plenty. If you are feeling as if life just isn't how you'd like it to be, take some time to acknowledge what's going right. Offer gratitude from deep within. From here you can begin to change your thoughts to a more positive outlook.

August 18

IT'S EASY TO GET LOST in distractions. The more energy we give to the things that keep us from focusing, the easier it is to stay distracted. Taking time to pay attention to what's most important to us will help us create, complete, and concentrate on our motivations. Make a list of all the things that distract you and then a list of what needs your focus. To make progress, choose what you will give your attention to today.

August 19

EXPLORE THE BEAUTY THAT is right outside your door.
Notice the tiny details that make where you live special.
Practice being present as you move through your day.
Take full deep breaths, smile at strangers, and pay
attention to what is in front of you. The only moment
that matters is right now. We can get so caught up in our
heads that we don't notice what's in front of us. When we
choose to be present, it's amazing how lovely and calm a
day can be.

———

August 20

THERE IS SOMETHING SPECIAL about anticipating the
blossoming of a flower. As the bud begins to develop, you
can see the firmly wound petals slowly bursting to the
surface. It is exciting to know that something remarkable
is about to occur—and worth observing. Then when the
blossom opens, you can appreciate its intricacies at a
deeper level because you waited. You are blossoming.
Be patient as your life unfolds. Soon you will see that
the waiting was well worth it.

August 21

SOMETIMES WE NEED TO FORGIVE, even when forgiveness feels impossible. When we hold on to a hurt, it only harms our souls. We can't change the other person but we can change how we react. The only thing we have control of is how we react and think. Don't allow resentment to take root and keep you from moving forward. Free yourself from the burden of pain by forgiving the person over and over until you're free.

August 22

IN THE DESERT, a palm tree is a reminder that growth is still possible. A grove of palms can hug tightly together along a stream, creating an oasis of shade in a harsh environment. Even when life feels arid and dry, things still grow. When it feels as if nothing is happening, below the surface it is. Over time, stillness produces growth. Know that wonderful things are coming to you. Be like a palm tree and choose to grow, even in the toughest environment.

August 23

WHEN YOUR INTUITION SPEAKS, it's unmistakable. Sometimes it's a gut feeling. Sometimes it's a feeling in your heart. Intuition speaks in different ways to each one of us. Take some time to locate how your intuition speaks to you. Listen to your inner voice and recognize your inner hunches or truth signals. The more you act on your intuition, the stronger it becomes. Eventually your intuitive cues will be unmistakable.

———

August 24

THE SUN'S WARMTH RADIATES through the fog. As it makes its way through, it warms the air and glimmers throughout the day. Uncertain circumstances can make us feel as if we are caught in the fog. Not being able to see the outcome can be frustrating. Notice the glimmers of hope when they appear and accept the ambiguity. Sometimes the mystery is the most amazing part of becoming. Let go of the need to control and know—and trust that everything is working out.

August 25

WHEN GRAPES RIPEN, they go through a process called
veraison. It's an incredible sight to see the berries turn
from green to purple. A bunch doesn't mature all at once
but creates a lovely pattern of color. In time the grapes are
ready to be harvested as they ripen in the sun. Changes
often occur in stages and it may not feel as fast as you'd
like, but know that in time the changes you seek will occur.

August 26

A WANDERER'S HEART is never satisfied. The longing to
see and do all that the world has to offer is their driving force.
They make stops along the way, sometimes for longer periods
than others. And yet their souls prod them to move on, to
continue to explore and seek new vistas. They're content in
their movement. They find peace in change. They see each
trial as a token of wisdom. The world is their home.

August 27

IF YOU'RE HOLDING TOO TIGHT to something, loosen your grasp. It is hard to let go when our minds and hearts want to hold on. Sometimes the only thing to do is release that grasp, which masquerades as the control we've already lost. Breathe. Accept. Be ready for what is supposed to enter your life. Let go. Make room for the new things you want to enter your life. When they appear, you'll understand why letting go was the thing to do.

———

August 28

THERE WILL BE PEOPLE who come into your life for a season and leave. It's not your job to try to keep them there. Sometimes we just need to move on and be grateful for our time with them and the lessons learned through that season. If you are missing someone today, send them love. Appreciate what they brought into your life. Forgive them if you were wounded when they left. Release the attachment you have to foster healing.

August 29

AS YOU GET READY FOR THE MORNING, repeat these healing words to restore your soul for a fresh start to the day: *I offer myself grace today. As I give grace when I feel undeserving, I open my heart to receive from others. I let go of judgments and fears for they no longer serve me. I welcome healing. Life isn't perfect and I can't expect myself to be. I release my expectations and embrace the blessing that is today. I welcome newness and possibility with open arms.*

August 30

OUT IN THE DESERT, a camel can sustain itself without food or water for weeks. To survive, it stores up energy for the harsh environment. A camel's ability to conserve energy and water helps it make journeys and sometimes carry heavy loads. This is a reminder that we all have inner resources. If we tap into our intuition, we can make difficult decisions, heal, and thrive. Even when we are going through something hard, what we need is available to us.

August 31

LEARN FROM THE WOUND; teach from the scar.
When you are going through a hard time, it can be enticing
to broadcast it for sympathy or commiseration. But if
you take the time to find the lesson from the wound, a
transformation can happen. Bless the wound and find
healing in the lesson. You can help others by teaching
from the place where restoration occurred. It becomes an
important part of your personal geography. Your wounds
offer a chance for deep healing and can eventually serve
as a glimmer of hope to others.

September 1

ONE OF THE MOST TRANQUIL times in a city is early
in the morning. As the sun rises, the buildings reflect their
gleam, painting the streets with a golden hue. There is
a stillness before the day begins and the streets fill with
people going their various ways. Even in the busiest of
cities, sunrise brings beauty and the opportunity to be still
and welcome the day from a place of peace. How will you
receive peace today?

September 2

WE LIVE IN AN ABUNDANT UNIVERSE. When you find yourself in a state of scarcity, think about a time when your needs were met. Remember how you felt anxious, wondering how it would all work out. Remember that it *did* work out. Be grateful for that time and the trust that helped result in that outcome. Tap into that feeling and clear the worry to allow space for whatever is on the way.

September 3

EVERYTHING YOU HAVE GONE through has brought you to this point. You are a survivor; you thrive and can emit your light, even though some others may not see the positive side of their situation. Our cracks are where our lights shine the brightest because of the energy we put into healing. Allow the healing in your life to be a lighthouse for others. You are proof that hope is alive.

September 4

HARD WORK CREATES RESULTS. The illusion of an overnight success can keep us frozen on the path to greatness. If things aren't happening as quickly as you would like, know that all your hard work will pay off. Check on your vision and make sure it's clear. The universe is conspiring to help you. Paint a clear picture of what you want. Show up. Do the work and then trust that the greatest good will occur.

———

September 5

IS THERE SOMETHING IMPORTANT you want to achieve but feel scared to go after? Courage is the antidote to fear. Great things take bravery. What are you on the verge of exploring, creating, or otherwise doing? Think about what your life would be like once you achieve it. Take the doubts and fears and breathe courage into them. One of the first actions toward actualizing your dreams is breathing in courage and breathing out fear.

September 6

BEFORE YOU BEGIN YOUR DAY, take some time to plan the way you want your day to go. Allow your mind to focus on this intention and visualize how you can incorporate it today. See yourself as you want to act, respond, and communicate. As your day progresses, remind yourself of your intention. An intention can be a guidepost for each day. If you feel off course, remember your vision and act, respond, or communicate from that guidepost.

———

September 7

EMBRACE BLISS! Life is to be enjoyed and moments of bliss are to be welcomed. When good things happen, embrace the moment and know that you are worthy of feeling this good. Breathe in the feeling of bliss and sit with the happiness. Be joyful. Staying present allows the joy to sink in and raises your energetic vibrations. Recall times of bliss you've experienced and the way you felt. Give gratitude for these moments in your life.

September 8

DISCOURAGEMENT CAN KEEP us from trying to move forward. But you're stronger than that. You are greater than the fear-based thoughts that plague your mind when you feel discouraged. You are a strong, capable, and talented person and can do great things. When you face a setback, get back up as quickly as you fell. You are resilient—and discouragement can quickly be turned into motivation to get up, move forward, and learn. You are becoming.

September 9

IT'S LOVELY TO WAKE early in the morning to see the moon set as the sun emerges. It's like a rite of passage, a changing of the guard. To know that there are two enormous orbs in the sky that ascend and set each day is a reminder that nothing is too big to overcome. Be like the sun and moon: work together with others to make the world a wonderful place. You don't have to rise and radiate light alone.

September 10

WHEN YOU STEP INTO your purpose, you are sending energy out to the universe, exclaiming, "I'm ready. I want this!" Your energy will be met with what is meant to transpire. Taking the first step toward your purpose is sometimes the hardest. If you are on the edge of taking that step but feel panic starting to set in, stop your mind from listing all the things that could go wrong and take the leap.

———

September 11

A GREAT TRAGEDY CAN bring people together. When bad things happen, some people rise to help in the midst of great sadness, wanting to help alleviate the pain. Concentrate on how you too can help and see the good that does arise in response to terrible events. We are not helpless when bad things happen. Agents of change show up in unexpected ways. Together we can bring healing energy to the residue of tragedy.

September 12

THE PATH TO SUCCESS is not straight and narrow. Many diversions, doubts, and mistakes happen along the way. Milestones remind you of what you are working toward. Celebrate the small successes you achieve along the way. When confusion and fear surface, remind yourself how far you've come. Keep looking toward your objectives and make moves every day to achieve your dreams. Be flexible and adapt to change. Your life is supposed to be an incredible journey.

————

September 13

CREATIVITY IS BOTH MAGICAL and practical. It is born from inspiration and develops through dedication and hard work. We are all creators and can inspire those around us. Creativity lives in each of our souls. When you tend to the spark within you, it can become a flame. When you choose to create, you access the part of you that has a primal need to make something out of nothing. Bring forth the creations within you.

September 14

WAITING FOR SOMETHING can be difficult, especially when it's something you desperately want. Sometimes our timing isn't what the universe has in store and we are called to be patient. While waiting we have a choice to feel hopeful or hopeless. Not getting what we want when we want it can be divine timing. We don't know what the future holds. Trust that everything is happening with perfect timing and surrender the need to know *when*. The answers will be revealed in due time.

September 15

WORRYING ABOUT THE DAY only invites anxiety. Today will go exactly as it needs to go. The only thing you can control is your reaction to the things that happen around you. If you feel anxious about something, spend a moment to reframe it in your head. Turn the negative thought into something positive and enter your day with fresh eyes and the resolve to react less and invite calm when anxiety begs to thrive.

September 16

AN ARTIST TAKES their time to create a masterpiece. Each brush stroke is important and adds layers to the depth of the image. The artist doesn't try to rush their work as they know that great works involve hours of attention and care. Your life is also a masterpiece and deserves great attention and care. Be patient as you work toward your goals. Honor all the work you are putting in. Your masterpiece will reveal itself soon enough.

———

September 17

AFTER A LONG SEASON OF GROWTH, fruit is ready for harvest. It's amazing what can grow from a tiny seed. A seed can generate an entire bounty. With proper care and nourishment, a plant will yield fruit for many years. Harvest is a reward for all the hard work and patience put into the plant's growth. We are like plants that go through seasons of growth, harvest, and rest. Notice what season you are in right now and honor where you are this season.

September 18

GROWTH CAN OCCUR EVEN in a harsh environment. A cactus flourishes in the desert by storing water for the driest seasons. It intuitively knows how to prepare for difficult times. We too can mentally prepare ourselves for such seasons by training our brains to be resilient. Every time you find yourself facing difficulty, look for the lesson. Find gratitude in the midst of stress and your brain will become more resilient. Then in times of struggle you will have the tools you need to succeed.

September 19

YOUR SPIRIT IS THE life force within your body. You are a beautiful being, and your feelings, personality, and essence make you who you are. Everything you experience is a way to feed your spirit. Some things nourish you while others drain you. To know the difference, notice how you feel with each experience. Your spirit is a gauge, a navigation tool to keep you alive and well. If something is depleting your life force, redirect your energy toward something more nourishing.

September 20

WHEN YOU'RE MET WITH ADVERSITY, respond with
confidence. You have what it takes to get through it. We
build perseverance by going through difficulty and surviving.
Even though it's hard and feels overwhelming, there is help
available to see you through. Tap into your inner strength and
ask for help from the universe and your network. We aren't
meant to face trying times alone. Reach out and upward,
and know that on the other side, you will be stronger.

September 21

ONE OF THE GREATEST LESSONS we can learn is to
soften during difficult times. At times we may shut down
and throw our protective walls up. But if we do, we will
stunt our own growth. The universe is always providing
opportunities for us to evolve into our fullest potential.
When we open up, soften, and allow things to flow, it's
amazing what can happen. Notice where you can soften
to let growth emerge.

September 22

ONE OF THE GREATEST THINGS you can give yourself is a belief in your abilities. Doubt can feel like a never-ending whirlwind. Negative thoughts weigh down hope and inspiration, keeping you from moving forward. Remember all the things you have been through and accomplished. You have achieved great things and can do whatever you put your mind to. Don't let doubt cloud your mind. This morning, affirm what you are capable of. You can do hard things and will accomplish something great today.

September 23

DO ONE THING THAT MAKES you happy today. Joy is all around. It's a lovely day and we can find joy every day. If you spend your time indoors, make sure to go outside. Spend some time in the sunshine, feeling the warmth on your skin. Do something out of the ordinary. It's so easy to get caught up in our daily schedules that we can forget to take time to feel happiness. Create the time to find it.

September 24

IN TIMES OF SORROW, IT CAN BE EASIER to shield ourselves from the flood of emotion by pushing them aside. When we grieve, we may not be aware of the gravity our emotions have if we don't allow the space and time to process them. There is relief in the release. Give yourself grace during such times and allow yourself to feel, to process, and to heal. Feel the flood disperse by allowing the tears to flow. Healing comes where flow occurs.

———

September 25

SEE THE GOOD IN YOUR MORNING and repeat these words for a positive day: *I am grateful for the sleep I just awoke from, and I welcome this day from a place of excitement. When I move through the day, I will find the goodness that is in front of me. I will greet others with a warm smile and let them know that I see them. I will offer myself love and acceptance. I am grateful for my body and the steps it will take. Today I choose to see beauty everywhere.*

September 26

AS THE SUN RISES OVER THE DESERT, it spreads its golden glow. The stunning yet stark scenery is illuminated, showcasing reds, oranges, and greens. Before the heat sets in, the cool morning air feels brisk, offering temporary relief from the sun's powerful heat. There is a tranquility to a desert morning. Even the harshest environments provide something alluring. When you face a harsh situation, look for the good in it and illuminate what is cloaked in darkness.

September 27

EVERYTHING YOU HAVE gone through has created a mosaic, colorful and rich. Each experience adds depth to your life, giving you greater awareness and understanding. You are a brave soul, and as you overcome hardship you become a beacon for others, glimmering hope in dark places. Continue to spread your brilliance bringing hope and love to those around you. The world is a better place with you in it.

September 28

SOMEDAY, EVERYTHING YOU WANT and long for will be your reality or a memory. Be present with where you are right now. Think about how far you've come and all the things you've done to get where you are. Take a moment to be grateful to your past self for wanting and longing for what you have now. Then release your grasp on what you want and long for, and trust that everything comes to you at the right time.

———

September 29

WHEN CONFLICT ARISES, do your best to go first, even when you don't want to. Say you're sorry. Let go of resentment. If the relationship is important, listen to your heart and quiet your ego. It's not always worthwhile to be right. Love can create a path to understanding. Invite more love into your life by giving love, even when it's hardest to give. In these times, trust builds and love grows deeper.

September 30

THERE IS POWER IN SAYING NO. Having too many things to concentrate on can keep you from giving your full attention to the task at hand. Place boundaries on your time and give yourself the space to breathe. Life shouldn't be lived in a vortex of stress and struggle. Review your to-do list and make note of what you can put off until later. You deserve to have space to focus, breathe, and create with a clear mind.

October 1

WHEN YOU SPEAK TO YOURSELF, be more like a cool breeze and less like a furnace of judgment. Give yourself love and accept yourself exactly as you are. Honor the journey you've been on with acceptance and appreciation. As you wake up, think about all the things you have accomplished. Give yourself gratitude and love. When you slow down to recognize who and what you are, acceptance comes in like a breeze, making everything better.

October 2

WE ALL HAVE A SPARK WITHIN US. It's made up of our charisma and energy. When we sparkle we can illuminate an entire room. Throughout our lives our spark waxes and wanes, like the moon. Sometimes we feel its warmth and other times it's hard to find. To keep your spark alive and well, do things that light you up. Allow yourself to shine and be seen. Do the things that set your soul on fire.

October 3

THE WIND CARRIES THINGS AWAY and brings other things closer. It doesn't think about the destination; it just blows where the current takes it. As the wind travels, it picks things up only to set them down in a new location. The wind doesn't hold on tight, because it knows that nothing is permanent. The spirit of wind is letting go. Be like the wind, releasing and receiving as needed. Be fluid, given that nothing in life is permanent.

October 4

FALL MORNINGS ARE CRISP AND FULL of color as the leaves reveal their true colors. The days are becoming cooler and everything seems to be preparing for winter's arrival. Just before the trees become bare and the ground freezes, there is such vibrancy to behold because for a short while, trees are their most vibrant color. Take the time to enjoy their stunning colors. Notice how each tree is different yet beautiful, and then do the same for humans. The world is full of diverse beauty.

October 5

WHEN DOUBT AND FEAR fill your mind, examine your thoughts to find the truth. Fear takes pride in throwing us off course. We can train our minds to recognize fear's voice and reframe our thoughts into something encouraging and hopeful. Stop and ask yourself, "What is the truth?" Important things often feel scary—and that's okay. You are brave and able to accomplish anything you set your mind to. Let hope and courage take the place of doubt and fear.

———

October 6

APOLOGIES CAN BE HARD TO MAKE. When we hurt another person, we have a choice to release the pain we've caused and offer healing or to hold on to the anger and allow bitterness to take root. Everyone must apologize at some point in their lives. Acknowledge the hurt. Offer the apology and then it's in the other person's hands whether to accept it or not. Do your part. Let go and move on. Saying sorry can be quite healing.

October 7

THERE IS A LIGHT WITHIN YOU that never diminishes and serves as a guide for others. When you feel as if your radiance has dimmed, take time to restore your energy. Rest and recharge. You are here to shine bright because the world needs you. And if you feel like dimming light for the sake of other's comfort, shine even brighter. There is no one like you. Permit yourself to brighten the places you need to. Glow on!

October 8

BE WILD AND FREE. There is a spirit inside of you that is primal. Let it flow—and reach for what fills your soul. Your intuition is the voice of your soul; listen to what you truly desire. Release any feelings of guilt or judgment. Allow your soul to speak its truth. Be open to your inner truth and allow your spirit to be your guide. Life should be joyful and exciting. Sometimes we need to set our primal nature free.

October 9

IN SILENCE WE CAN HEAR our intuition speak. But it can be difficult to find silence in the age of hyperconnectivity. We must make it a priority to find the time to unplug and create silence at least once a day. All of the information and connection will still be there when we return. A change happens when we learn to access stillness; we start to crave the quiet in the midst of all the extrinsic connection. In stillness we find our balance.

October 10

AS THE BUTTERFLY MAKES ITS WAY out of its cocoon, it struggles to free its wings, then eventually, after some time waiting, its transformation is complete. If you have been striving and working on something and just waiting for a result, keep going! Some good things take months or even years, but it's worth it. When you see the hints of transformation, your heart swells with gratitude because you know you made it work and it was all worth it. Keep going! You're doing amazing things!

October 11

TEARS ARE TEMPORARY. A healing release can occur when we let ourselves weep. Sorrow reminds us of the joy we once had, the love we've received, and the pain we've endured. By allowing tears to fall, we embrace the strength to emote and feel. It's not easy to allow our emotions to show. Vulnerability is a sign that you trust your feelings and are ready to process them. Embrace the flow of tears; they provide release.

———

October 12

ENDLESS OPPORTUNITIES ARE available to you. Life is full of experiences to be had, people to connect with, and abundant sights, sounds, and flavors. In a matter of hours, we can completely change our surroundings. If you feel as if you don't have enough, remember how infinite the universe is. Think about all of the choices we get to make every day. Focus on the abundance around you and transform scarce thoughts.

October 13

THE DAY BEFORE YOU is a mystery, with twists and turns that can bring fun and joy. When morning dread wants to take over, try to summon excitement. Seeing the day ahead as a mystery about to unfold opens our minds to possibilities. If you let each day offer moments of awe, it is easier to wake up with anticipatory excitement. See everything as a gift and open your eyes to the wonder all around.

October 14

START EACH DAY WITH A beginner's mind. As you awaken, let expectations fall away and approach the day open to learning and absorbing the wealth of information in store. From this place you can surrender to what you don't know so that you can learn. You are an explorer of truth and knowledge, and today holds a lesson for you to uncover. May you discover the treasure the day has in store.

October 15

AUTUMN IS A SPECIAL TIME of year, as the air becomes crisper and things seem cozier. Leaves are changing their colors; the temperatures drop, and the sun rises later. Harvest has been completed and part of the world is getting ready to settle into the cooler months when hibernation begins. Fall has a magical essence, with its vibrant colors, cooler air, and the completion of a season of growth. Reflect on how you've changed this year and celebrate your growth with gratitude.

October 16

WHEN YOU FIND A FRIEND who will listen to you, show up when they need you and provide feedback in a loving manner, hold them close. Friendships are to be cherished and nurtured. To have the type of friendship you desire, you must be that type of friend in return. Think about a friend who has been there for you and whom you trust. How can you extend friendship to them today? Show your love and appreciation with a heart full of gratitude.

October 17

THE MOMENT YOU WERE BORN, you took a breath and your lungs filled with oxygen, causing you to inhale and cry. You are alive! And every day since then, you have filled your lungs with air. Some days you have cried tears of joy and sorrow. You are meant to be here. Today is another gift to breathe, laugh, and perhaps cry. It's all here for you to experience and make it what you desire. No matter what you've been through, you are here and that's worth celebrating.

———

October 18

THERE IS A DEPTH OF knowledge within you and your experiences cultivate a deep wisdom. Your life is a road map, full of journeys your soul is bound to encounter. Dive into life with all your heart and soul. Let go of the need to understand everything as it comes. Each twist and turn deepens your understanding of yourself and the world around you. You are meant for greatness. Welcome your inner power and tap into the well of wisdom and your life will be extraordinary.

October 19

TODAY, GIVE YOURSELF SOME kindness and inspiration with these words: *I am a vibrant being, and I am here to make a difference. My purpose is unique. The world needs me to find my voice and share it. I am here for a reason. Today I choose to step into my power and embrace the wonder of being alive. I choose joy over discontentment. I am ready to show up and share my greatness. I am ready to make today mine.*

———

October 20

DEEP WITHIN MOUNTAINS, crystals can be found. Deep in the ocean, an exciting world appears. Deep in the soil, roots dig down to support the giant trees our eyes behold. Appearances aren't what they seem. There is always something deeper and enchanting to be uncovered through discovery, patience, and trust. Our souls are the jewels that lie deep within. Get to know others on a deeper level to witness the charm within them. There is always much more than what meets the eye.

October 21

LIFE IS FULL OF CHOICES and opportunities. When we are presented with options, it can feel overwhelming. If you have a big decision to make, don't pressure yourself into deciding immediately. Take your time to do the research. Give yourself the freedom to ask the questions that you have. When you've gathered all the data and taken some time to think, you can make the decision from a calmer state of mind.

October 22

THINK ABOUT A TIME WHEN someone offered you true empathy. Didn't it feel comforting to be seen and heard? Empathy is a healing emotional balm. Being able to understand and share the feelings of another person creates connection. We all have times when we need to give and receive empathy. Be present with others and hear what they are expressing and feeling. Offer genuine understanding. Practice empathy often with loved ones and notice how your heart connection grows.

October 23

IF YOU WERE TO BE TRULY honest with yourself, how would you answer the question "Am I becoming the person I want to become?" If the answer is anything but yes, dig deeper and ask yourself, "Who do I want to become?" Every day we can create the reality we desire. It doesn't always mean big sweeping changes, but it could mean choosing a different path, meal, activity, or thought. Whatever it is you really want, do something today to bring yourself closer to it.

———

October 24

THE PURSUIT OF PERFECTION is a losing battle because nothing will ever be perfect. Since everything is consistently changing, it would be impossible to try to make something permanent. We do this with ourselves, our children, our friends, our jobs, and even where we live. When we live in a state of acceptance, we can come to terms with things just as they are. There is always room for improvement, yet perfection is an unreasonable goal. Aim for better and then accept what is.

October 25

YOU HAVE A BEAUTIFUL MIND, capable of amazing things. Choose to expand and reach for what you want. Don't allow fear to take over and cause you to contract and accept a smaller life than what you deserve. You are worthy of your biggest dreams; go out and experience life to the fullest. Life happens when you step outside your comfort zone and push yourself to find a new level of comfort.

October 26

OPEN YOUR ARMS AND welcome abundance into your life. The universe hears your deepest desires. You are ready to receive. If your thoughts are focused on what you don't have, that will be your reality. The best part is that we live in an abundant universe. Let go of the thoughts of not having enough and open your mind to the possibility of everything working out and the abundance of joy that's on its way to you.

October 27

ON COOLER MORNINGS, it feels inviting to stay in bed
a bit longer. Stepping out from under the covers to start
the day can also be invigorating. Our thoughts create our
reality. Enjoy the warmth of the covers as well as the rush
of starting your day. Be grateful for the comfort of your bed
and the sleep you just had as well as the cool air and the
start of a new day. There is a good side to everything.

October 28

A BIRD DOESN'T WORRY if it's aiming too high; it just flies
by instinct. Soaring above the clouds, hovering over the
oceans, birds are a symbol of freedom and perspective.
When we desire freedom, we must relinquish control.
To soar high, we have to let go of the limiting beliefs we
hold on to because they provide the illusion of control.
Step back and see the horizon, and then take a leap into
freedom, allowing the higher perspective to be your guide.

October 29

A MOUNTAIN STANDS TALL and sturdy high above a river that flows and is ever changing. This juxtaposition mirrors the complexity of nature. At the foot of a mighty rock face, a river can erode the power and grandeur of the rock. Just as life continues to flow no matter how tall and strong you are, life will cycle through to refine and erode hard layers. There is beauty in strength and in weakness. Embrace both parts of you.

October 30

LIFE IS FULL OF OBSTACLES and we get to choose our paths. Almost everything we do is by choice. Whether we choose the right path depends on our outlook and ability to right the course if it seems wrong. When faced with a decision, take some time to tap into your intuition and find your inner compass. You already know the answer. It lies deep within you. Listen closely and your soul will speak its truth.

October 31

CELEBRATE YOUR ACCOMPLISHMENTS every day. We get so busy trying to achieve that we can forget to pause and revel in what we have already achieved. There are so many things that are worthy of recognition. Spend some time each day acknowledging what you have accomplished, big and small. Then show yourself some appreciation for the effort you put forth. Share your wins with someone and celebrate together.

November 1

WHAT A WILD AND INCREDIBLE LIFE you have created. Every step you've taken has led you to this moment. Nothing was a mistake. Your perseverance helped you get through the hard times and your inner light guided you through life's storms. Now here you are, ready to live another day in your extraordinary story. Today is just another page in the epic adventure of your life. Enjoy everything this day has to offer you.

———

November 2

THERE'S ALWAYS ANOTHER SIDE of the story or perspective to be considered. By doing this, we focus on compassion and empathy. If you are facing a difficult situation with someone, try to see it from their perspective. This doesn't mean you have to agree; it just allows compassion to enter and perhaps solve some parts of the conflict. We are doing the best we can with the tools we have. Let go of resentment by trying to see the other side. Imagine what healing would occur if we all did this for each other.

November 3

WATER IS AN AMAZING SOURCE of life and power. Start your morning with a glass of water to wake up your body. As you shower, feel the sensation of the water cleanse your skin. If you live near a body of water notice the depth it contains. When it rains, recognize the replenishment it provides to the ground. Water is everywhere and desperately needed in many places. Appreciate and respect the abundance of water in your life.

———

November 4

TO LIVE WITH INTENTION MEANS deciding how you want to feel and why—and then making an effort to radiate that in your actions. A shift happens when we live intentionally. Peace, calm, purpose, joy, contentment, and trust are just some of the amazing results. But like any process, it's a practice. Once you begin to live with intention, you will be able to live a life of deeper meaning and purpose. How do you want to feel and why?

November 5

AFTER IT RAINS, SOMETIMES THE SUN comes out and
rainbows appear. Take a moment to stand in the presence
of a rainbow in awe, looking up at the sky that just released
the rain. Remind yourself to always look up because
there is always hope, inspiration, and wonder to behold.
So today, look up and see the sun shining and notice what
is taking place. Acknowledge the appeal each day brings and
remember that hope and wonder are always within reach.

———

November 6

THINK OF ONE PERSON WHO has made a difference
in your life. Now take a moment to hold them in your heart
as you send them loving vibes for the day. See them happy,
fulfilled, and at peace. Offer gratitude for their presence
in your life. Feel the love and gratitude reverberate through
your body. Now do the same for yourself. You too deserve
the love and appreciation you just offered to that special
person; you are just as special.

November 7

WHEN THINGS SEEM TO BE falling apart and nothing is going as planned, breathe. In times like these, all you have control over is your reaction and your breath. Focused breathing relieves tension and makes you aware of where your body is holding tension. Send breath to those parts of your body and feel yourself release the tension that can surface when you acknowledge your lack of control. Letting go of the way you'd like things to go and sinking into the flow will invite peace and acceptance.

———

November 8

TREAT YOUR HEART WELL today and every day. Seek and strive for what your heart and soul truly want. Listen for intuitive cues to your purpose. Whatever you choose to do, do it with all your heart. The vibrations you emit when you are fully engaged are higher and attract like energy toward you. Even if it's a mundane task, if it moves you closer to your ambitions, put your heart into it. Your heart will surge with pride and love.

November 9

UP IN THE TREES, A CROW CALLS OUT. The crow has much to say and communicates until its message is heard. Crows are symbolic messengers of the gods and are believed to have a spiritual connection. As their call is heard, their message spreads. Each of us has a spiritual calling deep within. It's important to communicate our soulful messages. Tap into your higher self and listen for your calling. Use your voice to communicate your own message.

November 10

OPPORTUNITIES COME AND GO. The universe is plentiful. Just look at nature and all of its abundance. Rain comes after a drought. Wildflowers burst with color after a cold, bleak winter. There are countless grains of sand and every snowflake is different! When you feel "there isn't enough" or "nothing is available," reframe your thoughts and notice that abundance is all around you. Empower yourself by noticing the goodness that surrounds you. You will always be taken care of.

November 11

WHEN YOU START WORKING toward an objective, unseen forces are at work. The energy you put toward your goal is met by the energy of the universe. Taking action is sometimes the hardest part. If you feel stuck because your objective seems daunting and you don't know where to start, think of one small thing you can do to begin. Put your energy where you want to see growth. Eventually something will align and you will be glad you started.

November 12

LIFE IS EASIER AND MORE ENJOYABLE when we allow it to flow. Resistance blocks the flow in our lives. When we resist, what is meant to leave stays and what is meant to arrive is blocked. Notice any areas where you may feel resistant or stuck. Visualize removing that block and letting the good flow in and the bad flow out. Become open by releasing the need to control. Allow wonderful things to come to you.

November 13

VIBRANCY EMANATES FROM the inside out. How we think, feel, eat, and treat our bodies affects how we radiate. Take a moment and scan your mind, body, and soul and notice if there is anything hindering your glow. Are there big or small changes you can make to radiate your light just a bit brighter? Become conscious of your thoughts and how you treat yourself. Your light is magnificent.

November 14

TODAY IS THE PERFECT DAY to show appreciation. Go through your day with mindful gratitude for everyone and everything. In a season of thanksgiving, it can be easy to overgeneralize gratitude. It is one of the most powerful emotions and when we practice it, it can raise our energetic vibrations. As we give thanks, we train our brains to see the positive side of things and of others. Give appreciation wholeheartedly and feel your heart send out love with each thought or expression of thanks.

November 15

GRACE COMES WHEN we least expect it. It's everywhere if we look for it. That is the beauty of giving and receiving grace. When we feel as if there is nothing left and no more rope to hold on to, grace sweeps in and offers the support and love we crave. Some of us carry heavier burdens and wounds than others and need the relief that grace can provide. Give grace today to someone who deeply needs it. Your day will become brighter.

November 16

MOVE TOWARD WHAT YOU WANT with fervor. Step into your greatness. Let fear melt away as you take a step closer to the life you desire. Right now, you don't need to be afraid because everything you need is attainable. Stop playing it safe. If you find yourself complaining about the same thing over and over, change it. Only you can make your aspirations come true.

November 17

YOUR FOCUS CREATES YOUR REALITY. When you have a dream that you hold near to your heart, try seeing it as if it's already happening. Notice how it makes you feel. Recognize the work you put into getting there. Breathe in gratitude. As you go through your day, return to this vision for inspiration. Know that you are working toward this incredible goal. Each focused step brings you closer to a new reality.

———

November 18

NO ONE IS EXACTLY LIKE YOU. It's amazing to think that each one of us is different because of our minds, bodies, and souls. We are here with a distinct purpose and imprint that won't be duplicated. Celebrate what makes you different: you are special just the way you are. Notice and celebrate the differences in others. Find the awe in diversity that each of us contributes to the world.

November 19

YOU ARE MEANT TO ENJOY LIFE. Nothing is permanent. If you are going through a transition, think about the joy that will come when you get through whatever you are dealing with. Your soul becomes stronger with each change. Find adventure during this time. Enjoy the new vistas and memories you are making. Happiness is always available to you. Let go of the way you think things need to go and relax into the journey.

———

November 20

WHEN HARD TIMES HAPPEN, look for the glimmer of hope and the presence of grace. Even when difficulties arise, there is goodness to behold. Grace sticks out because it's given even when we may think it is undeserved. Time and again we are giving and receiving grace from the universe, and from there hope takes root. Look for the silver lining, for all storms come to an end. After the storm passes, new life emerges. Something new is awaiting to enter your life. Let it be.

November 21

YOU ARE AMAZING and your dreams matter. Struggling doesn't have to be the go-to mode in your life. You are here for a reason. There is a purpose to your life. Even if it's not clear what it is, your soul knows. What if you paid attention to your deepest desires and gave them room to breathe? Imagine if you took a step to make these dreams come true and the courage that would build by taking that jump into your destiny!

————

November 22

THERE IS A SOFT BEAUTY in receiving and accepting. Sometimes it can be difficult to receive gifts, praise, or help. When we resist and don't accept, we deny ourselves the energy of worthiness. Life is a balance of giving and receiving. When we give, it feels incredible. The same can be said of accepting if we allow ourselves to soften into it. Practice receiving today. When someone compliments you or extends assistance, simply say "thank you." Notice how it feels to receive and not resist.

November 23

CONCENTRATION CAN FEEL elusive when it feels as if all the tabs in your brain are open. We live in an endless loop of information. Although this is convenient and awesome, it takes a toll on our nervous systems. To function at our highest capability, we need to take time for stillness. Start your day shutting down all the tabs in your brain and finding your center. Let peace enter if only for a moment. Breathe in the stillness.

———

November 24

YOU HAVE EVERYTHING you need to get through what you are facing. Resources are available and your resilient spirit and mind can figure things out. Don't allow fear to take over and tell you it's impossible. Don't allow fear to paralyze you from moving forward. You can and will get through this. On the other side is freedom from what's weighing you down. Just think of how amazing that will feel. Keep going—you've got this!

November 25

WELCOME STRENGTH INTO YOUR DAY with these affirmations: *I accept that life is full of uncertainty, discomfort, heartache, and pain. I am strong enough to handle it all. I grow through discomfort and become a better version of myself. Every trial that I overcome ignites my warrior spirit. My courage and strength are always accessible. When I think I can't do it or overcome, my inner strength rises up, making me bolder than before. I am courageous and strong.*

———

November 26

TO BE LOVED, WE MUST GIVE LOVE. We have the opportunity to send love to others every day. We can send love in word, thoughts, and actions. Give love without expectation. Send love to the people you pass on the street. Do something nice for the people you live with. Love when it's hard to love just as much as you love when it's easy. Create a spirit of love every day and notice how your life transforms. How will you love today?

November 27

LIFE IS A GRAND ADVENTURE. If we knew what
was around every corner, life would be dull. The ups
and downs make life richer. You are brave and equipped
for the adventure your soul is supposed to experience.
There is nothing too great for you to overcome. Support and
other resources are out there to help you along the way.
Think about a time when you overcame something that felt
daunting and how you not only survived but thrived.

November 28

CHOOSE TO TAKE THINGS a little slower today. There
is no need to rush. Life happens at the pace we choose.
Welcome the *joy of missing out* into your life and take in the
moment and place you are in. Sometimes the only company
you need is your own. Seek solitude in your slowness to
find answers within. Just for today, allow your pace to be
unrushed and notice how much more you remember from
your day when you spend your time more mindfully.

November 29

THE BRANCHES OF AN OAK reach outward and upward toward the sky. Its branches are like tentacles—some gnarled, others straight as if they are floating midair. The oak always reaches for greater heights and wider horizons. They are a spectacular sight to behold—strong, sturdy, and expansive. Be like the oak and never stop reaching. Always stretch yourself further and when you think you've reached enough, keep reaching. There's no telling where you'll end up.

November 30

OUR LIVES ARE MADE UP OF CYCLES. Everything comes and goes in a cyclical manner. The quicker we embrace the cycles in our lives, the faster we can accept what is. Just like a river flows through a canyon, we too must allow life to flow, holding loosely to what we have because it is only passing through. Today, give gratitude for all that is in your life and open up to all that wants to flow into it.

December 1

EVERY DAY WE HAVE A CHOICE about how we want to feel and what we want to do. Choice requires consistent awareness of how we are feeling and how we want to change until it becomes habit. That's why each day we can choose to take a step toward forming new habits. Choose a theme each month to create a new habit. Because habits are formed with time and practice, imagine the growth and change that can take place in a year. What will you choose today?

December 2

AS THE SUN RISES IN THE FOREST, it shines through the canopy of trees. The dew on the forest floor casts an earthy scent as the ground warms up. Birds chirp in their nests up high as they prepare to search for food. As the forest awakens, it welcomes the sun, which reveals the intricacies of the forest as the shadows become enlightened. Be like the forest and let the light seep into your shadows so you can awaken.

———

December 3

TRAVEL OPENS OUR MINDS to people and stories that we wouldn't experience at home. Our planet and fellow human beings are awesome. We can learn from so many different perspectives and see so many places. Even venturing to another town or city nearby can open our minds to something new. When we stay in our comfort zones, we don't let ourselves expand. Expansion allows magic to happen and pushes us to grow. Invite magic into your day by doing something or going somewhere different.

December 4

AS WINTER APPROACHES, notice what didn't grow this year alongside what blossomed and flourished. Focus on the things that thrived and not what wilted. Release what didn't thrive and celebrate what transpired. This is a season to reflect, release, and make room for what is meant to grow in the spring. Celebrate what grew as well as what failed. What was meant to be flourished. Things happen in due time and there is peace in that truth.

December 5

HOLDING ON TO HURT can cause suffering. When we focus on the pain, bitterness, resentment, and sorrow, anger can grow. When we choose to let go of the reaction to hurt, we feel freer to focus on the good in our lives. Don't be lured by the false comfort that commiserating gives us. Choose to focus on something positive and feel your body change. Release the hurt, let go of suffering, and feel yourself become lighter.

December 6

WHEN WE HAVE HEATED DISCUSSIONS with others and problems emerge, it's common for us to react from a place of judgment. Judgment and pain come from low vibrational energy that only fosters negativity. Instead of approaching a problematic situation with a harmful reaction, release judgments and extend warmth and understanding. When we experience a lot of hurt, healing can only be fueled through higher vibrational acts like embracing gestures of love and kindness.

December 7

WHEN THE DAYS BECOME COLDER and the sun takes longer to rise, it can be easy to become lethargic. It's easy to stay inside when the days are shorter. But each day has the same number of hours and life continues. If you feel like it's difficult for you to rise today, think of one thing you'd like to accomplish. Then move through your day with that one goal in mind. Rise and seize the day.

December 8

YOU ARE THE WRITER of your story and you get to
choose the meaning you give to the events in your life.
If you allow yourself to adopt the narrative of a victim, that
is the energy you will attract. True empowerment comes
when you choose to change the narrative into something
that helps you climb up above the struggle and tap into your
resilience. Rewrite your narrative and take your power back.

———

December 9

IF YOU ARE GOING THROUGH a period of sorrow, it can
feel all-consuming. Let go of the pain and bitterness that
holds you back. By holding on we create suffering. Forgive
yourself and others. Accept what happened and choose to
move forward, free from the grip of suffering. Breathe in
forgiveness and breathe out suffering. Forgive and free
your heart from the pain so that the hurt is released, and
joy can enter.

December 10

LIGHT SHINES THROUGH a stained-glass window, painting a rainbow of color on the wall. Without the sun's light, the colors look less vibrant. The window's beauty is more apparent when it is illuminated. We too are more vibrant when we allow our inner light to shine. Don't let your light be dulled by circumstances. You can still shine when things are hard. Your soul is a beacon to bring you back to joy and remind you that you have everything you need.

December 11

IMAGINE BEING OUT ON THE WATER first thing in the morning. Everything's quiet and even the wind is at rest. You are looking to the east and watch the horizon light up with the rising sun. The place where the ocean meets the sky begins to become more distinct as the sun brightens the sky. The water sparkles in the sun's presence. It's a stunning sight to behold. All is well and a new day has begun.

December 12

DURING A STORM, the ocean is choppy and unsettled. Deep down, there is a calm that isn't as tumultuous as the surface appears. The same happens when we go through hardships in our own lives. We may seem okay on the outside, but our inner world can be as unsettled as the ocean. Eventually all storms pass. If you are feeling a lack of control and the chaotic urges that result, let go and release. This storm will pass.

———

December 13

COMPARISON CAN KEEP US FROM experiencing happiness. Where you are right now is exactly where you need to be. Worrying about what others are doing takes your attention away from the present moment. If we spend our days comparing ourselves to others, we rob ourselves of the opportunity to lead a fulfilling and happy life. When you find your mind comparing, bring it back to the moment at hand and find something about yourself that you are thankful about.

December 14

THE STORIES WE TELL OURSELVES can either empower or weaken us. When we live in our heads, we don't appreciate the current moment. Sometimes we are so busy crafting our stories that we miss the importance of what is happening right now. Take a moment to stop, take a breath, and notice everything that is happening. Appreciate what is and allow what is going to happen to enter naturally into your life.

December 15

GRATITUDE IS AN ANTIDOTE TO STRESS. When you're feeling overwhelmed, it's easy to allow fear to take over. Stressful thoughts can lead to anxiety, and at times keep us from moving forward. By simply stopping for a moment to interrupt these thought patterns with gratitude, you can alleviate stress. Sometimes all we need is to stop and redirect our thoughts. The more you can find moments of gratitude, the easier it is for your mind to release fearful, anxious, and stressful thoughts.

December 16

PEOPLE COME AND GO throughout our lives. We make friends and lose friends in cycles. Some people are meant to be in our lives for a season and others for a lifetime. Each type of relationship is valuable, because each soul we encounter is a gift, offering us a lesson. Reflect on your relationships today and give thanks for the lessons and for the souls you've been able to meet in your lifetime.

———

December 17

WHEN MORNINGS BECOME COOLER and the sun takes a bit more time to make it over the horizon, we go inward. As winter approaches, nature begins to rest. After a year of growth and producing, plants and animals slow down and store up their energy. Take the time to slow down to restore your energy. It's okay to take breaks. Take a cue from nature and let go of the need to overproduce.

December 18

HOW SWEET LIFE CAN BE when you allow it to be easy. Letting go of resistance and embracing the lessons that come with each struggle and reveling in victories are part of the ride. Learning to allow things to come and go can be one of the hardest lessons because we crave control. But the lesson shows us that surrendering to *what is* makes life richer. When you feel the urge to resist, remember that on the other side of the resistance is a new level of comfort.

December 19

OUR HEARTS SWELL WITH LOVE when we give to others. Think of a mother and how she gives a part of herself to her children. She is filled with love for another the moment she gives birth. This love reaps rewards that she could never have imagined. This love helps her when hard times appear and moves her to give beyond what she thought she was capable of. When you give in love, you realize the capacity of your heart. Give with love and notice the expansion of your heart.

December 20

CHOOSE TO HAVE AN AWESOME DAY. Let your mind dwell on possibility instead of negativity. By choosing to find possibility, you will infuse your day with hope. This optimistic approach will make you feel lighter. Challenges are unavoidable, yet our outlook is the only thing we have control over in such times. As you rise, spread brightness on what is dark.

———

December 21

TIMING IS EVERYTHING. When things don't go the way we want them to, there is a reason. We learn so that we can grow. Our souls thrive when we look for the lesson in each situation. When we choose to complain and resist, we feel pain and can become stuck in its spiral. Trust that in time the reason will reveal itself. Stay open and find contentment with where you are right now.

December 22

YOUR BODY IS INTELLIGENT and provides clues about what it needs. When we are in touch with our intuition, we can easily pay attention to the clues our body provides. By tapping into our inner wisdom, we can live a healthier and more vibrant life. Nourish your body and mind today. Pay attention to what your body is telling you. Make your health a priority and show your body deep respect and appreciation.

December 23

CHANGES ARE INEVITABLE, and when we try to resist them, we only create stress for ourselves. The stress we create is avoidable if we release our grasp on what we think should happen. When you are going through a season of change, try to see the excitement and promise of something new. Letting go of what we know can be painful but holding on to what no longer serves us is even harder. Clear space. Something lovely is on its way to you.

December 24

BEGIN YOUR DAY WITH these expansive mantras:
I am choosing to expand and prepare for the growth that is about to take place. My life is not meant to be lived on the sidelines, watching and waiting. I am becoming an active participant in my life, open to learning, growing, and accepting lessons as they appear. I am growing and pushing aside old beliefs that no longer serve me. I am ready to take up the space that was meant for me.

December 25

TO CREATE A RICHER LIFE, gather your tribe and let them know how important they are to you. Spending time with our tribe fosters connection and understanding. Life is designed to be shared, and when we identify the people who make our lives better just by being in it, we foster a sense of belonging. A tribe can be as little or as large as you desire. Choose those who uplift, inspire, and interact with a spirit of love.

December 26

THE ROAD TO SUCCESS is not a straight line. Along the way we encounter many dips and curves, including failures. When the road gets difficult, the key is to right your course as best as you can. Getting up after each failure builds the resilience you'll need today and in the future. This journey and all its lessons were aimed for you, and you are becoming wiser and better equipped with each obstacle you overcome.

December 27

OUR DIFFERENCES MAKE US unique and the world needs your presence. Even if you feel as if something has been done before, your perspective and approach make it important that you share your gift with the world. Don't worry about what others think; you aren't here to please everyone. If you put your mind on doing your best and showing up, those who need you will find you and appreciate what you have to offer. Serve your purpose, not the masses.

December 28

IT'S EASY TO CREATE MEANINGS that correspond to the feelings we experience. If we are feeling upset, the meaning we give the situation can be frustration. The same can be said if we are feeling happy, we can create a positive meaning for that experience. We have the power to change our interpretations of situations into something empowering. If you feel yourself in a loop of negativity, try to find a positive meaning to each situation. Empower yourself and embrace the situation for what it is.

December 29

COMPASSION MOTIVATES US to help others in need. Compassion takes us a step further than sympathy by awakening the desire to alleviate pain and suffering. When we don't know how to help, we can look for ways to extend our compassion. Sometimes just sitting with someone who is hurting and creating a loving space for their pain is enough. Notice where are you drawn to help. Then ask yourself how you can express and demonstrate compassion.

December 30

SET INTENTIONS WITHOUT EXPECTATION. Expectations create disappointment when they aren't met. It's difficult to see past an expectation when we hold it tight in our hearts and minds. To find peace and contentment, it's important to let go of expectations. We can strive to live with intention, but if we have expectations about our intention, we may set ourselves up for great disappointments. Give up the desire to have things a certain way and allow things to unfold.

December 31

AS OUR MINDS REFLECT on the completion of another year, we focus on what we accomplished and our plans for the upcoming year. Take a moment this morning to bring awareness to the current moment: it is the only thing that matters. All your to-do's can wait. All that you are planning will happen in due time. In this moment, offer yourself gratitude for getting to where you are today. You made it! Give gratitude for a year full of beauty, lessons, and love.

Acknowledgments

Writing a book takes a lot of time and energy, and I am so grateful for my husband, Nate, who has patiently been by my side for three books now. Thank you for your encouragement when I doubt myself, abundant love, and excitement as I make my dreams come true. Your support means the world to me.

To my publisher, Rage Kindelsperger, thank you for your faith in my writing and taking a chance on me a few years ago. I am honored by the opportunity to share my words with the world. I will always have a special place of gratitude in my heart for you.

To my editor, Keyla Pizarro-Hernández, you are a rock star and so good at helping me make my words sound even better. Thank you for your eagle eyes, guidance, and collaboration on this manuscript. I am so happy we were able to work on another book together!

Making a book look and feel beautiful is an art and the design team and Quarto are the best at what they do. Thank you for infusing your talent into this book.

To the designer, Kim Winscher and Creative Director, Laura Drew, I am honored to have my words next to your gorgeous design work. To the cover illustrators, @spacefrogdesigns, when I first saw the cover, my heart skipped a beat because it was just so perfect!

To my family and friends, my life is richer with each of you in it. I am grateful for all the love, support, and encouragement you have given me over the years. Thank you for being the best tribe a gal could ask for. My heart is full of love and gratitude for each of you!

About the Author

Emily Silva quit her corporate job in 2014 to pursue her dreams of becoming an author and starting her own business. She launched a coaching company that specializes in helping women harness their bravery to bring their gifts into the world. She helps her clients with career changes, starting their own businesses, and cultivating their spiritual lives. She lives with her husband in San Diego when they aren't traveling to create their next soul adventure.

She is the author of three books: *Moonlight Gratitude, Find Your Glow, Feed Your Soul,* and *Sunrise Gratitude*. To learn more, visit her website soulsadventures.com and follow her on instagram @soulsadventures.

Also by Emily Silva

Moonlight Gratitude
365 Nighttime Meditations for
Deep, Tranquil Sleep All Year Long
ISBN: 978-1-63106-292-6

Find Your Glow, Feed Your Soul
A Guide for Cultivating a Vibrant Life of
Peace & Purpose
ISBN: 978-1-63106-641-2

First published in 2020 by Rock Point,
an imprint of The Quarto Group,
142 West 36th Street, 4th Floor,
New York, NY 10018, USA
T (212) 779-4972
www.Quarto.com

Rock Point titles are also available at discount
for retail, wholesale, promotional, and bulk
purchase. For details, contact the Special Sales
Manager by email at specialsales@quarto.com
or by mail at The Quarto Group, Attn: Special
Sales Manager, 100 Cummings Center,
Suite 265D Beverly, MA 01915, USA.

10

ISBN: 978-1-63106-695-5

Library of Congress
Cataloging-in-Publication Data

Names: Silva, Emily, author.
Title: Sunrise gratitude : 365 morning
meditations for joyful days all year
   long / by Emily Silva.
Description: New York, NY : Rock Point, an
imprint of The Quarto Group,
   2020. | Summary: "Sunrise Gratitude offers
a collection of 365
   thoughtful meditations to encourage you to
have joyous mornings"--
   Provided by publisher.
Identifiers: LCCN 2020012100 (print) |
LCCN 2020012101 (ebook) | ISBN
   9781631066955 (hardcover) | ISBN
9780760367742 (ebook)
Subjects: LCSH: Gratitude--Meditations.
Classification: LCC BJ1533.G8 S55 2020
(print) | LCC BJ1533.G8 (ebook) |
   DDC 179/.9--dc23
LC record available at https://lccn.loc.
gov/2020012100
LC ebook record available at https://lccn.loc.
gov/2020012101

Publisher: Rage Kindelsperger
Creative Director: Laura Drew
Managing Editor: Cara Donaldson
Project Editor: Keyla Pizarro-Hernández
Cover Illustration: @spacefrogdesigns
Interior Design & Layout: Kim Winscher

Printed in China